The

MALE
GAZED

On Hunks, Heartthrobs, and
What Pop Culture Taught Me
About (Desiring) Men

MANUEL
BETANCOURT

Catapult
New York

First Catapult edition: 2023
First paperback edition: 2024

Hardcover ISBN: 978-1-64622-146-2
Paperback ISBN: 978-1-64622-222-3

Library of Congress Control Number: 2022922958

Cover design by Dana Li
Cover photo © Edward Cordoba / Stocksy
Book design by Laura Berry

Catapult
New York, NY
books.catapult.co

Printed in the United States of America

10 9 8 7 6 5 4 3 2 1

Praise for **THE MALE GAZED**

Named a Best Book of the Year by NPR, *Time*, and *Them*

A *New York Times Book Review* Editors' Choice

"*The Male Gazed*, by the queer Colombian writer and film critic Manuel Betancourt, is a smart, refreshing essay collection on the subject, and deals directly and honestly with the paradoxes surrounding the topic of men . . . It's delightful, and perhaps cathartic, to see Betancourt turn the tables on masculinity by returning its gaze . . . A welcome perspective on a thorny, timely subject. Readers are sure to leave with a useful lens through which they can give masculinity a second look."

—JOHN PAUL BRAMMER, *The New York Times Book Review*

"Manuel Betancourt explores queer representation in media in an intensely personal, and uniquely engaging, manner. He recalls a childhood in Colombia as a 'soft and skinny' kid whose ideas about masculinity were shaped by a host of disparate influences . . . Betancourt finds the through line of forbidden desire connecting them all and unpacks how his life as a writer and a gay man exists in an ever-evolving conversation with their notions of manhood." —NPR

"How does one manage to intertwine astute observations on gender with a heartfelt recounting of 'staring agog' at Gaston in 1991's *Beauty and the Beast*? Writer and critic Manuel Betancourt knows, and does so masterfully . . . As much as *The Male Gazed* is a riotous trip through a media memory lane, the book also provides an opportunity to rethink our ideas about masculinity as a whole, and to embrace new ways of talking about intimacy, identity and gender roles." —*People*

"Hilarious and provocative." —*Cosmopolitan*

"*The Male Gazed* . . . untangles the simultaneous threads of desire to be a beautiful man, or to be with beautiful men, then unravels the implications of all of it to understand how those threads form the self. Betancourt is a preeminent thinker . . . who brings true intellectual rigor to his analysis of contemporary media."   —*Esquire*

"One of the joys of Betancourt's expansive writing is how it invites readers to make their own connections, to slot their associations into the frameworks he presents as he fluidly examines a wide array of media . . . Both criticism and memoir, the book holds no straightforward answers but insists that uncertainty and ambiguity are, in fact, the point."   —*Them*

"*The Male Gazed* is a necessary and compulsively readable dissection of how pop culture both reflects and creates the world around us."   —*Slant*

"Betancourt (*Judy Garland's 'Judy at Carnegie Hall'*) makes gender theory both accessible and fun . . . What he uncovers may be just enough to begin salvaging a robust and dynamic sense of masculinity from the toxic strains that have become so prevalent in social discourse."
—DAVE WHEELER, *Shelf Awareness* (starred review)

"In this sharp, sexy, and sparkling collection of essays, Manuel Betancourt leaves no rock-hard stomach unturned as he investigates how the most popular televised and filmic images of idealized masculinity are constructed, disseminated, and devoured by queer men, himself included. *The Male Gazed* is both history and his story: Betancourt deftly oscillates his critic's eye between the screen and the self too, reflecting on an upbringing in Colombia colored by swooning telenovelas and Disney's G-rated hunks, twinks, and twunks; on an adulthood in North America studded with friends turned lovers and lovers turned friends; on queer futures being made manifest in the present. Betancourt is a dream critic—as in, a fabulous scholar of dreams, of the desirous imagination."
—MATT ORTILE, author of *The Groom Will Keep His Name*

Also by Manuel Betancourt

Judy Garland's "Judy at Carnegie Hall"

To all the men I've gazed at from afar and especially those who've let me do so at closer range.

Contents

The
MALE
GAZED

1.

Once Upon a Dream

I HAVE A MEMORY OF SEEING DISNEY'S ANIMATED FILM *Sleeping Beauty* in theaters. Or rather, I think I have a memory of it. My mom loves to tell the story of me watching *Sleeping Beauty* so much and so often that I must have conjured one from her stories, feeding it details I couldn't possibly remember as an impressionable eight-year-old. In any case, in this memory, I am so enthralled by the moving pictures that as soon as I come home, when my uncle asks me how I liked the film, I proceed to (in painstaking detail, of course) retell it in its entirety, with the kind of flourish only a shameless young boy could pull off. I mimic Aurora's dance with her woodland creatures. I hum along to her signature song. I even use some makeshift props to better portray the movie's devilishly stylish villain. It's quite an involved performance. More of a recreation than a simple retelling.

"And then the prince gave her the kiss of love," I inform my uncle toward the end, as if he'd never heard this story before, "and woke her!"

It's understandable why my mom so enjoys telling this story. It appeals to her ideal image of her firstborn: fearless and sociable, he's a consummate performer. In truth, he's a bit of a drama queen. Apocryphal as it may have become, the anecdote was a staple of family conversations as I grew up, an origin story of sorts for my own self-described obsession with the movies. Revisiting the film now, I can see why its flattened medieval tapestry of an aesthetic beckoned me to walk toward this simple (and simplified) fairy tale and bring others along for the ride.

But this film, whose jagged angles and curlicue designs pushed against the rounded confines of its traditional romantic narrative, also served as an early lesson about who I was and who I was expected to become. My flailing about as I tried to emulate the film's two central female characters—one demure, the other fabulous—stood in stark contrast to the way I all but purposely ignored the dashing Prince Phillip. He was a portrait of masculine stoicism. His rigidity was made all the more apparent by the fluid movements of the female characters around him, leaving me little to play with as I performed the film for a rapt audience of one. More simply: Prince Phillip is the most boring character in the entire thing. But there was, perhaps, another reason for my reticence to impersonate him. I preferred to stare at rather than be him, an early indication that I would become more comfortable gawking at men than playing at (or with) them.

I wouldn't call what I felt for Prince Phillip *lust*, but there was something to how my eyes lingered on his slim, alluring body, especially when he was seized and tied up by Maleficent's minions, muzzled lest he call out for help. But my gazing, even at that age, startled me. I remember sensing I needed to watch him from afar, to keep myself at a distance lest my closeness to who he was and how he made me feel inspire other, equally discomfiting thoughts. Already I saw myself becoming a mere spectator of the very thing demanded of me: Phillip's male brio was unattainable. More than that, it was utterly uninteresting. Here was a part that would only ever be a performance for me. And if I was to perform, I would rather indulge in the more fascinating figures that flanked him. This was the first of many instances in which the silvery images on-screen kindled a growing realization that maybe I wasn't like other boys.

Disney properties encouraged many such moments of self-reflection in my childhood. And, because of their continued ubiquity in my adulthood, I can't escape the ways they shaped me. Ever since I watched *Sleeping Beauty* up on the big screen, I've been haunted by what these fairy tales taught me, and how I, in time, have had to unlearn and reshape myself in their wake. Even as a precocious eight-year-old, for example, I knew that a line about how someday a prince will come, how someday I'll find my love, wasn't meant for boys like me. Yet, before I could grow up and further question the gendered roles modeled in films like *Snow White and the Seven Dwarfs* and *Sleeping Beauty*, I saw in that lyric a sense of possibility. Perhaps one day my prince *would* come. Such childish fantasies, so rooted in sincerity and optimism, meant these animated flicks had some secret magic that could encourage a young queer boy to take both transgressive and imaginative leaps. Given that Disney's fairy tales were so intent on enshrining heterosexual "happily ever afters," it's unclear if these childhood moments in darkened theaters predicted the gay man I would become, or if I have simply warped them to do so in my mind. The result, I guess, is no different either way.

Everything I know, after all, I learned from animation.

I don't mean to sound glib, but I do truly owe much of my up-bringing to hand-drawn fairy tales, *Looney Tunes*, and many a *Silly Symphony*. Animation, so often misunderstood as mere childish entertainment, is irrevocably tied to didacticism. With its exaggerated facial expressions and elastic character designs, animation can teach a kid a lot about themselves and the world around them. Everything from anger (Donald Duck) to smugness (Bugs Bunny) can be traced within a few animated lines, sometimes without even needing a hint of dialogue. Moreover, animation traveled well across borders. Growing up, Colombian TV channels aired American animated shows and Japanese anime series in equal measure, often with the same dubbed voices that helped flatten them both in my eyes (or ears, I guess). Whereas the process of dubbed foreign content irked me as a wholly insufferable bilingual fifteen-year-old eager to practice my language skills, I could let it slide when watching animated fare—this was a medium well suited for such transnational export.

But the quip is also a nod to the fact that, since my mom runs an animation studio in Bogotá, everything I did learn growing up led back to hand-drawn sketches, watercolor backgrounds, scattered storyboards, and the soothing hum of scanners in her office. This is the world I grew up in. With my siblings, I spent way too much time cooped up at her studio, finding new ways of entertaining myself whenever she had to work weekends to meet a deadline. Besides splitting time on the one dial-up-enabled PC I had to share with my siblings and watching subtitled American sitcoms on cable channels we didn't have at home, my weekends at the office often included hours spent poring over coffee table books like *The Art of Hercules: The Chaos of Creation* and *The Art of The Lion King*. It was through watching my mom's animators work and by reading these various tomes (and watching any and every behind-the-scenes featurette that aired on the Disney Channel) that I learned how painstakingly intentional every element of animation filmmaking truly is. Drawn in by such artistry, I began to think of myself as a budding critic.

My mom, who'd earned a degree in preschool pedagogy, found herself using much of what she'd learned at school in her role as co-owner (with her boyfriend) of Colombia's very first animation studio. She was particularly proud of the work she did in producing short animated videos about homegrown inventions for Colciencias, a government agency tasked with supporting applied science and technology research. She understood firsthand the way animation could key into childhood curiosity and impact children's worldviews; it's an argument that has regularly kept animation confined to G- and PG-rated fare, a limit case for how theorists, parents, and even legislators have understood the power of cinema on seemingly all too impressionable kids.

From 1929 to 1933, shortly after films entered the lives of everyday Americans, the Motion Picture Research Council set out to investigate the impact this newest mode of mass entertainment was having specifically on children, as they were, notably, the first generation to grow up with moving pictures as part of their popular culture diet. Cinema's ubiquity—it is conservatively estimated that in 1934, there were roughly seventy-seven million weekly movie spectators in the United States alone!—was cause for celebration, yes, but as studies showed, for alarm as well. The worry was that what kids were watching would not only influence them, but maybe—to use writer Henry James Forman's word—"mold" them entirely.

Forman's 1933 book *Our Movie Made Children* set out to answer the question everyone was asking themselves at the time: "Are the movies good or bad for my child?" Forman's pivotal book cited and amassed much of this budding research and arguably set the tone for the way in which cinema's (albeit unintentional) didactic impulse would be understood for decades to come. Admitting that the research he'd assembled in his book was still speculative at best (cinema having barely been around for a generation), Forman arrived at the kind of conclusions that feel self-evident and simplistic: "movies tend to become a school of conduct for children and adolescents," he writes. Forman hedges his argument before openly saying that watching crime films will undoubtedly sway children toward a life of crime; there was too little research to suggest that, and maybe just as much to dispute it, but he firmly believed in the power of the movies to corrupt, an argument he put in front of his readers in hopes they'd assess the research he'd provided and, perhaps, come to a not dissimilar conclusion themselves.

What's remarkable about such a polemic is how familiar it remains nearly a century later. Decades before I could flippantly note that yes, movies did indeed help me become the gay man I am today—making me a "movie-made gay" as I often describe myself—a slew of curmudgeonly social scientists were framing such a statement in alarmist tones that ushered in the kind of pearl-clutching hysteria that has characterized conservative views on the ill-advised influence of popular culture on children around the world.

Which is why, despite Forman's unquestioned influence on our conversations about how movies can shape a young child's mind, I gravitate instead to Parker Tyler. If Henry James Forman seemed stuck in the past—he was born in 1879 in Russia—Parker Tyler's ideas were unabashedly modern. Born in New Orleans in 1904, Tyler grew up never having not known about the movies. And while he never intended to become a film critic (by 1933 he'd already cowritten *The Young and Evil*, an experimental novel about Greenwich Village that was indebted to modernist writers like Djuna Barnes and Gertrude Stein), cinema became central to his work as he broke apart the mesmerizing power it had over him.

"Why do we go to the movies? Most every intelligent person puts this question to himself at one time or another, often repeatedly and disgustedly, and always out of a sense of shame. It's the modern version of the medieval query: Why does man sin?"

Henry Miller first wrote those words for a preface to Parker Tyler's 1944 book *The Hollywood Hallucination*. After reading Tyler's monograph, one of the very first to seriously consider cinema's artistic possibilities, the *Tropic of Cancer* author was convinced he needn't bother writing about Hollywood as he'd long wanted. Tyler had beat him to it. Miller's conflation of movies, shame, and sin when discussing Tyler's prose is not coincidental. Central to Tyler's understanding of cinema was the conviction that there was something almost erotic about being engrossed in a film. He imagined moviegoers as daydreamers who had a hard time distinguishing between the darkness of the theater and the darkness of their own bedrooms. To read Tyler's delightfully campy prose is to get lost in a world where Hollywood is both mythic and visceral, a near-biblical experience, easily sliding from knowledge to sex and right back again.

Given their outrageous vision of cinema, Tyler's books—with titles like *The Three Faces of the Film: The Art, the Dream, the Cult* and *Sex Psyche Etcetera in the Film*—have never quite become the classics of film criticism they deserve to be. Part of this has to do with Tyler's idea of a consummate moviegoer. "The spectator must be a suave and wary guest," he writes in *The Hollywood Hallucination*, "one educated in a profound, naïve-sophisticated conspiracy to see as much as he can take away with him." This is an image of a spectator that traffics in contradictions. Or who, better yet, exists within and across opposing ideas like naïveté and sophistication. They're eager to steal what they can from those visions on the screen. It's a portrait of a spectator as a young burglar. Movies weren't, for Tyler's spectator, mere mirrors or windows for personal self-reflection; they were banquets from which to pilfer ideas, images, and a myriad sense of self. There's agency in his image of the moviegoer. For a young boy like myself, for example, who didn't quite understand why images of brave princes weren't just boring but ill-fitting outfits, cinema could also be an arsenal ready to be plundered, which would help me through the moments I spent outside of those darkened theaters.

I return to this decidedly queer approach time and time again because it helps me understand what my seemingly glib childhood obsession with Disney means to me now as a thirtysomething-year-old gay man. Tyler's wild theories give me a template to untangle what it is I've stolen from Disney's oppressively heterosexual fairy tales and, over time, how I've smuggled queered meanings from within their straitlaced happily ever afters, making them central to how I think of myself.

It's no surprise that I have had to reach into film criticism's margins to find a kindred spirit. Whether couched in the alarmist tone of Forman's studies or enshrined in highbrow critiques of Hollywood as a self-serving dream factory, the notion that movies could teach you what it meant to be a man—a gay man, even—seems laughably obvious at best and absurdly pedantic at worst. Tyler was perhaps a tad too hyperbolic in treating Hollywood films as modern-day myths, equally as powerful in helping us understand the world and ourselves as the stories that riddled Mount Olympus back in ancient Greece. But there is something to be said about the queer ambitious spirit Tyler brought to bear on his work. Nevertheless, despite being a contemporary of Bosley Crowther and James Agee, two of the most influential film critics of the early twentieth century, Tyler and his theories have become all but footnotes in the history of film criticism.

It didn't help that by 1968 he'd become the butt of the joke in one of the most controversial books the late sixties produced: Gore Vidal's *Myra Breckinridge.*

The novel's opening lines—"I am Myra Breckinridge whom no man may possess. Clad only in garter belt and one dress shield . . ."—don't really prepare you for what's to come. The outrageous plot of this now camp classic follows its eponymous protagonist as she arrives in Los Angeles hoping to claim her late husband Myron's inheritance. This requires Myra to confront Myron's uncle, an aging Western star who runs an acting school in sunny California. And so, while Uncle Buck has his lawyers investigate why he's never heard of his nephew's wife ("he was a fag or so I always thought"), Myra is hired to teach at Uncle Buck's school, where she advances her outlandish theories about the power of 1940s cinema to influence a generation of men. She also unabashedly flirts with the school's most coveted young stud (part of, as she confides in the reader, her master plan to "possess men" in order to conquer their gendered world), all but stealing him from his girlfriend, a fellow student who turns to Myra for comfort. The novel only gets crazier from there, especially as it careens toward the inevitable climax when Vidal finally reveals the truth of what happened to Myron.

From her conception, Vidal's protagonist was mythical, exceeding the imagination of her own creator. In his memoir, the famed author admits that what became the novel's opening line took possession of him: "The voice roared on. Who was she? I could only find out if I kept on writing. She was obsessed by Hollywood movies. That was soon clear. No matter how kitsch a film she could swiftly penetrate its mystical magical marshmallow core. Even so, it was not until I was halfway through the story that I realized she had been a male film critic who had changed his sex; Myron had become Myra. Why? I wrote on, laughing."

Just as initial reviewers focused on what *The New York Times* referred to as the novel's "standard gamey bits"—*Time* magazine wondered whether literary decency had fallen so low or whether fashionable camp had risen that high—later critical conversations of Vidal's text have centered on Myra's sexual and gender ambiguity. This was further encouraged by the way the 1970 film adaptation was derided because of its unabashedly queer sensibility. Exemplary of the offensive language and critical lambasting the film was subject to, the *Newark Sunday News* stated, "the picture has an anal fixation that will please only a fag audience." The film was disowned by Vidal himself, and by much of its cast. Most infamously, film critic Rex Reed, who played Myron in the film, published a picture essay skewering the film and its troubled production in the pages of *Playboy* to coincide with the film's release.

Even in the most scathing reviews at the time, you can sense how the film's outrageous sensibility deepened and complicated what the famed author had first envisioned when he dreamed up Myra. In his negative review of the film, for instance, critic Joe Rosen points out that, "What was anal in the book is banal in the movie." This delectable turn of phrase gets at precisely why Vidal turned to Parker Tyler when first concocting this most ludicrous protagonist. Myra wasn't just a devout student of Tyler's writings—she became an instantiation of his ideas, especially when it came to how cinema shaped young men, queer and straight alike. With a desire to create a raucous wild satire, Vidal had turned to Tyler because his writing was, in his words, "wonderfully pretentious." And so in crafting his heroine, he arranged for her to be closely aligned with Tyler's ideas.

Vidal could've targeted someone like Pauline Kael, but in his mind, Tyler was "more camp," as he put it, "and further out," which was endlessly more amusing to him. The author hoped to create a character whose ideas about the movies were necessarily preposterous, a symptom of a budding blabbering critical establishment who looked at films with awe and read into them anything and everything. Vidal—who had actual experience making Hollywood films, perhaps most famously with his rewrites of 1959's *Ben Hur*—was a pragmatist. Movies told stories. There wasn't much else there. Not myths. Not metaphors. Just stories. It's why Myra feels so outsized; like Tyler, she was interested in the collision and collusion between moviegoing and sexuality.

Moviegoing was a practice that Tyler located in an intimate and sexually coded bedroom; it's an idea that finds itself trickling down to the way Myra couldn't think of cinema without tapping into its erotic undertones. As a burgeoning young film critic, we are told Myron wrote an extended treatise on the buttocks of Western stars ("from austere aspiring Gothic flat ass Hoot Gibson to impertinent baroque ass James Garner"), and, as a devotee of Tyler and the male body, Myra agreed that she'd always been excited by men's rear ends, "possibly because it is in some way involved with my passion for 'backstage,' for observing what is magic from the unusual, privileged angle."

Such a line cannot help but echo Tyler's own project, which tied the erotic to the critical. For Myra, who was fascinated with the cinema produced between 1935 and 1945, those men on the big screen held the key to what she saw as her mission when it came to thinking about (and conquering) men (and their buttocks): to "re-create the sexes and thus save the human race from certain extinction." This hyperbolic assertion is couched in her conviction that cinema's postwar output had slowly destroyed American men. Without actors like Clark Gable and Jimmy Stewart ("godlike autonomous men"), Myra felt men across the United States had been left to "compensate by *playing* at being men, wearing cowboy clothes, boots, black leather, attempting through clothes (what an age for the fetishist!) to impersonate the kind of man our society *claims* to admire." American masculinity, in Myra's eyes, had been hollowed out into a fetishistic oppressively heterosexual performance, something so easily donned that its very essence had been lost. Her own emphasis on the supposed admiration suggests a schism between the image of men being projected on the screen and the type of man society *actually* admired.

Myra is here to tear down that cowboy masculinity she sees in the movies, a vicious and violent one she understands as misleading young men in the 1960s; it's why she seeks to "possess" (and penetrate, literally) the young stud in her class. Not only does she insert herself into a boy who is a "throwback to the stars of the Forties" and who reminds her of James Craig "in the fourth reel of *Marriage is a Private Affair*" (the film that coincidentally had first awakened young Myron to the sexual thrill of both its leading man and his leading lady) but she does so, bizarrely for sure, on a mission of the "destruction of the last vestigial traces of traditional manhood in the race in order to realign the sexes." This crazed rhetoric is what makes Myra (and Vidal's intentions in writing her) so hard to pin down: Is she violently destroying the image of inviolate masculinity so as to pierce it and deliver it into a new, queerer future? Or, in forcing such submission, is she paving the way for a return to retrograde understandings of gender, to the ways of men like Stewart and Gable? Vidal, a consummate satirist, makes answering these overlapping and interconnected questions even harder; rather than letting his protagonist run wild and succeed, he destroys her, depicting a vision of a future that seems just as jarring to a neo-conservative as it would to a radical queer.

At the end of the novel, our deliciously witty protagonist is mysteriously run over, and due to health complications, loses their silicone breasts. It's what finally pushes them to go back to being Myron, which lets Vidal sketch a queer riff on a happily ever after that involves Myron marrying a young girl (the young stud's girlfriend, no less), becoming a Christian Scientist, and getting a job at Planned Parenthood.

It's no surprise to see how being associated with such a novel derailed Tyler's reputation. The critic was so irate when he read the book that he swore he'd one day get his revenge ("I don't know what form the revenge took," Vidal quipped decades later. "And then he was dead."). With gleeful verve, Vidal had skewered Tyler's fanciful rhetoric, making it almost impossible to take the critic's insights seriously, even as the novelist's leading lady puts forth the most lucid explanation of how postwar ideas about American masculinity were both tied and indebted to Hollywood's output. This may explain why it's taken decades for us to take Tyler's concept of moviegoers looting films for self-fashioning purposes at face value. What else was I doing as an eight-year-old when playacting as a villainous diva if not finding bits of myself up on a screen many times my size? Films like *Sleeping Beauty* and *Snow White* weren't—couldn't really be—mirrors that I could find myself reflected in. But they did offer glimmers of possibility about what kind of man I wanted. And what kind of man I wanted to be.

Growing up in the 1990s, I didn't have those Jimmy Stewart and Clark Gable films (nor the Westerns Myra so despised) to introduce me to what an all-American man could be. For starters, I was born in Colombia and couldn't have cared less about such jingoistic imagery. Having always understood the United States not as a center of historical gravity but as an imposing centrifugal force that aimed to bend everything to its will, I was always inclined to take its exceptionalism as Hollywood mythmaking at best. Westerns, thus, continue to bore me, even as they remain fertile ground in which to deconstruct what alternative modes of intimacy can look like—just ask Ang Lee or Jane Campion, who've both refashioned what rugged, Western manhood can do to hardened cowboys. What I did have instead was a slew of films that were instrumental in my generation's own self-fashioning that, stripped of any one kind of nationality (they dreamed up, instead, fanciful cosmopolitan vistas from around the world), became as didactic as those studio films Myra so loved.

It's hard to overstate the cultural impact *The Little Mermaid* had when it was first released in November 1989. The Walt Disney Company, which hadn't animated a fairy tale since 1959's *Sleeping Beauty*, was taking a gamble with this twist on Hans Christian Andersen's story about a young mermaid who falls in love with a landlocked prince. For decades, the Mouse House had pivoted away from animated musicals and had found itself unable to recapture the magic that once made Walt's pioneering productions cultural touchstones. But by the time Ron Clements and John Musker's adaptation of this beloved classic made it to the big screen, it seemed impossible to imagine Disney animation doing anything else. The animated tale got great reviews and became the biggest box office hit the company had had in a decade. It then went on to win two Academy Awards, thus cementing its arrival as a watershed moment in Hollywood history. The Disney blockbusters that would follow—including *Beauty and the Beast*, *Aladdin*, and *The Lion King*—all owe their existence to the breakout success of Ariel and her friends.

What's striking about *The Little Mermaid*, a film whose VHS tape I almost wore out growing up, is the way it was underestimated by its own studio. Famously, Disney Studios chairman Jeffrey Katzenberg initially balked at green-lighting the idea and later believed the film, due to it not being a "boys' movie," would be less successful than the animated film he hoped would reignite the studio's animation roster, an anthropomorphic take on Charles Dickens's *Oliver Twist*. But *Oliver & Company*, which starred Joey Lawrence and Billy Joel as, respectively, an orphaned kitten and a carefree mutt, stands now as nothing more than a 1980s curiosity. Meanwhile, Clement and Musker's "girls' film" defied all odds and became an instant classic that has since spawned direct-to-video sequels, park attractions, a Broadway musical, and even a live-action remake. Katzenberg's hedged appreciation of the film's box office prospects does speak, though, to the gendered way in which we understand stories about young girls who get their happily ever afters.

Yet despite their unwavering focus on young women's experiences, these films, like *Sleeping Beauty* before them, created a space where cultural ideas of manhood and masculinity were perpetuated. There's a reason there's a Disney Princess line and no clamoring for an equally robust take on the company's many princes. And so, just as I had done with that disposable idea of a bland Prince Charming in *Sleeping Beauty*, I usually tossed aside the many iterations of that character. Eric may have a good head of hair, but I connected more with Ariel, who wants to be part of his world; Aladdin may have a slim waist, but it was Jasmine whom I found myself drawn to, especially in her quest to see a whole new world; and while Beast becomes a tender-hearted fuzzball, there was no getting around the fact that I saw myself in that bookish outsider Belle, who felt more at home in the pages of a good story than her quiet little town.

Then came Hercules, a character whose mere mention will always push me to think of the one line of dialogue that stopped me in my tracks: "So, did they give you a name along with all those rippling pectorals?"

I was twelve years old and thankful that I was in a darkened theater so my mother couldn't see how much that line made me blush. I had, in fact, been mesmerized by said pectorals. This was 1997 and

here again was Disney making me aware of my uncomfortable relationship with the male body. In my defense, and as Megara's dry-
witted mockery showed me, I was all but required to notice, covet,
and perhaps even lust after Hercules's pectorals. Sure, his biceps had
just bulged so much that they'd broken a measuring tape. But it was
his pecs you noticed. They were covered up by armor whose Ionic volutes guided your eyes toward them. They are what made Herc one of
my earliest big-screen crushes. And what made Megara, who inquires
about his voluptuous body so offhandedly, one of my most enduring
teenage role models; here at last was a Disney heroine who had no
time or use for men (or so she thinks). Old-school Disney classics
like *Snow White* and *Sleeping Beauty* trained me to pine for a prince,
boring and stoic as he may be; but as I came into my own and entered
puberty, these more modern animated films asked me to go further.
They encouraged me to thirst after their male protagonists and, sometimes, their fetching villains too.

I didn't need to have read Parker Tyler's theories about suscepti-
ble moviegoers or have encountered Myra Breckinridge's histrionic
lectures on Hollywood's masculine anxieties to key into the ways my
erotic attraction to these animated men spoke deeply about how it is
we're trained to view men on-screen and what happens when those
expectations are disrupted. I just had to find myself staring agog at,
say, *Beauty and the Beast*'s hunk of a villain or *The Little Mermaid*'s
silver fox of a father to see what my gaze told me about myself. After
all, like Herc, these were characters who looked like they'd grown out
of a gay man's animated wet dream. Where Aurora's Prince Phillip
was a waif of a lad (quite G-rated and thus better suited to my eight-
year-old self), these more modern Disney men looked like they were
on steroids. They were all bulging pecs and towering torsos. Gaston,
for instance, the local alpha male in 1991's *Beauty and the Beast*, is
the kind of man you'd find boasting about his latest bench-pressing
personal record at the gym, his body well-suited to a *Physique Pictorial*

centerfold if only he'd swap his hunting gear for a thong. He elicits his fair share of swooning for his overdeveloped upper body (as one song tells us, no one has a neck quite like his), an attribute that marks him as the epitome of what we, or Belle rather, is supposed to find attractive (it's why the swooning triplets don't understand why Belle doesn't immediately succumb to his charms). Triton, meanwhile, whose luscious white beard and flowing locks remind us where Ariel got her enviable head of red hair, has the kind of pronounced six-pack, rock-hard nipples, and V-shaped upper body you'd expect more from a bodybuilder in Venice Beach than a father figure in an animated film. Sharing the distinction of being some of the few male Disney characters to show off their chests with pride, they echo the kind of titillating "dirty" photographs the Finnish artist known as Tom of Finland used as basis for his stylized and highly masculinized homoerotic fetish art. These weren't just (animated) men one pined away for; these were men who gleefully invited our gawking gazes, insisting we imagine a less PG-rated type of "happy ending." Oh, to think what Myra and Tyler would have made of these visions of masculine splendor!

Not coincidentally, all three of these characters (Triton, Gaston, and Hercules) were designed and animated by Andreas Deja, a detail that might explain why my younger self was so drawn to these three animated men. Deja, an openly gay Polish-born German American animator, drew inspiration from what he knew best: there were ready-made templates for such parodies of masculinity surrounding him in Los Angeles. Yet, the stories behind these creations reveal an even more complex way of thinking about why they teeter on suggestive pinup boys. For instance, Deja remembers how, in coming up with the design for Gaston, he had to focus on making him more and more handsome. Katzenberg himself pushed Deja in this direction to better visualize the central theme of the movie: don't judge a book by its cover. Over the course of the film, the dashing young hunter would emerge as the true monster of the story, more of a beast than the fanged creature up in the castle. Turning to bodybuilders for reference, Deja juiced Gaston up. That this dashing villain originally had a mustache not unlike that donned by Kake, Tom of Finland's fictional gay leatherman, perhaps helps you dream up what kind of men Deja was encountering in late-1980s LA.

Similarly, when trying to design Hercules (a departure for Deja, who's also responsible for Jafar in *Aladdin* and Scar in *The Lion King*, arguably two of the most queer-coded male villains in Disney history), Deja struggled with how to make this young hero visually interesting. As Gerald Scarfe, the famed artist the directors Musker and Clements brought in to supervise and set the tone for the design of their film, put it, "Hercules was most difficult—the good-looking ones always are. In fact, Hercules is such a very handsome hero that with him, I could just suggest this rather hugely muscular figure who's not the cleverest guy in the world." Deja eventually found a way to marry Scarfe's stylized lines with Grecian motifs (ergo the volutes on his armor and on his curls), creating a lovable himbo of sorts who could be as playful as he could be strong. Those choices, about how big Gaston's biceps should be or how long Herc's neck needed to be, spoke to the way an animated character carries within them information about who they are. And while the voice work clearly helped elevate these various hunks, there's no denying that Deja's attention to their bodies was instrumental in making them feel real.

Sadly, much of that body language, in Disney flicks at least, depended on romance. Every storyline required a boy and a girl, a meet-cute, and a happily ever after. Think of Ariel smiling forcefully at Prince Eric, or Belle cocking her head at Beast as she sees there may be something there that wasn't there before. These were fairy tales that hinged on love. Rarely was there room for lust. For thirst. Unless you were looking for it, that is. Or found it waiting there for you, as if all you needed was to know where to seek it. There may be no hint of sexual chemistry between, say, the beauty and her beast (theirs is

a story of tenderness, of all-knowing glances and dancing sequences),
but the film's bulked-up villain nudged us toward the thought of these
characters existing in a world full of sexual beings. Gaston reads as a
perfect distillation of patriarchal masculinity. Not only is he first described as "a tall, dark, strong, and handsome brute!" but his encounters with Belle focus on his inability to see her as a woman with any
kind of agency, one who could have any dreams beyond becoming his
wife. "Belle, it's about time you got your head out of those books and
paid attention to more important things . . . like me!" he tells her, "It's
not right for a woman to read—soon she starts getting ideas . . . and
thinking."

Gaston is a textbook example of a bullying kind of misogyny
wrapped in gentlemanly concern. Not coincidentally, he's also a
character whose sexuality is front and center. His unabashed narcissism and exhibitionism meant that a G-rated animated film could
include a line that reminded us that every last inch of him was covered in hair as an image of his furry chest took over the entire frame.
To this day, that moment astounds me in the way it begs viewers to
imagine what else is as hairy as Gaston's pectorals. You have to imagine lyricist Howard Ashman, who'd worked on *Little Shop of Horrors*
off-Broadway and *The Little Mermaid* with composer Alan Menken,
had a ball trying to capture what it was that made Gaston such an
enthralling, if arguably loathsome, character. Ashman was openly gay
and died from AIDS complications before he could collect his second
Best Original Song Oscar (for "Beauty and the Beast"). He had to
know what he was doing; the lyrics for "Gaston" have the film's villain
boasting how good he is at spitting all while reminding us that no one
else "shoots" like Gaston. Similarly, Hercules's body was created to be
displayed and, like Gaston's, imagined as useful for one thing alone:
to save the girl. The workout montage that turns a scrawny Grecian
kid into a goofball of a gym bunny is aimed at getting Herc to save a
D.I.D., a "damsel in distress" in the film's Greco-contemporary lingo.

Not that there were that many of those to save. In late twentieth and early twenty-first century Disney films, women protagonists are anything but damsels, even if they are constantly in distress. With such female empowerment came, perhaps, an unintended consequence. The male gaze, which turns female protagonists into images and bodies meant solely for men's consumption, is mostly absent in these more recent films. Or rather, it's turned into something else. Think of the French triplets who sigh and faint whenever they catch sight of Gaston, or Meg's calculated-turned-authentic swooning for Hercules. These moments all shift the audience's gaze. As Disney gave its female heroines agency in their desire, it also allowed audiences to objectify its male characters.

Gaston and Hercules. It does not escape me that these textbook cases of socially sanctioned masculinity (hailing from eighteenth-century France and ancient Greece, though filtered through an American pop cultural sensibility) ended up serving as gateway crushes for a young Colombian boy who was as soft as they come. These characters embodied what I craved and what I feared. The bully and the jock were more than mere tropes to me. They were real-life schoolmates who constantly humiliated me and would have scoffed at my own inability to be anything more than a maricón pining away for animated men who felt accessible precisely because of their irreality. But that didn't stop me from wanting them and possibly wanting to be like them. What wouldn't I give, even all these decades later, to have Gaston's swagger or Herc's pecs? Or barring that, at least an ounce of the confidence they found in their own bodies?

That thin line between admiration and aspiration has followed me in the ensuing decades. I've looked to men around me, in screens both big and small (and sometimes in the real world as well) for guidance on what kind of man I wanted to become. It wasn't just that I had few pop cultural role models that didn't embody a constricted vision of masculinity. It was that I was enamored by it—by that vision of manhood those Disney characters embodied. This seemingly childish interest has morphed, over the years, into a critical inquiry. That moment with my uncle when I all but ignored the bland Prince Charming up on the big screen feels now like an origin story for this project, a first step toward recognizing how much cultural and personal power such images can have on kids, queer and straight alike. For those of us who consider ourselves "movie-made" gay men, heirs apparent to Tyler and Myra's queer vision of moviegoing, we do so because, as Stanley Cavell puts it in his seminal film criticism book *The World Viewed*, in so inviting movies into our lives, they "become further fragments of what happens to" us, like "childhood memories whose treasure no one else appreciates, whose content is nothing compared with their unspeakable importance." At a time when our notions of masculinity feel ripe for reexamination, I keep returning to those childhood obsessions of mine because, like *Sleeping Beauty*, they awoke in me an awareness about the kinds of stories we tell ourselves and the characters we're taught to root for, even to lust after; about the lessons we've taught young boys and about the expectations we have for grown men.

2.

Wrestling Heartthrobs

My LEAST FAVORITE SUBJECT AT SCHOOL WAS, WITHOUT A doubt, physical education. Every trimester, when I got my report card, I'd look aghast at that one subpar grade sullying my otherwise stellar record. In other classes I could study harder and read ahead. I could cram for exams and spend hours on special projects. I could practice math problems and review chemistry equations. But when it came to P.E., there was little I could do to excel. For starters, in keeping with that image of an insufferable bookish nerd you probably have in your mind already, I was pathetically unathletic. That was on top of being impossibly skinny and disappointingly short. When my entire class was lined up by height to better stage the group photo for our first communion ceremony, I was but third in line. That was still the case when we were lined up for our graduation picture seven years later. Secondly, our P.E. exams were graded on a curve. So, unless all of my very athletic schoolmates suddenly bombed their flexibility trials, fell during their speed laps, or somehow missed the mark on the rest of the Olympics-like tests that made up the bulk of our final exam grades, I had little chance of acing the class. I will say that in a bit of premonitory gay body awareness, the only physical tests I aced were the sit-up challenges;

I was already fixated on the rippled ridges that framed men's lower torsos—even, or especially, my own.

If I'm being honest, though, what kept me from truly wanting to do well in P.E. (or, as I phrased it back then, why I didn't *care* to do well) was the way it forced me to grapple with my body—and the bodies of my schoolmates. Our P.E. uniforms (tracksuits with matching tees and shorts, sponsored by Adidas, naturally; this was a private school, after all) were designed to cover us up. With no locker rooms, or anything like them, we just shed the tracksuit at the bleachers before we were set to play soccer, or volleyball, or whatever other sport we were assigned (much to my own chagrin, I could never join the all-girls gymnastics-but-really-merely-aerobics module). No, my glimpses of teenage boys' bodies came—as so many other things in my life—courtesy of American television. I first fell in love with obliques by ogling *Daria*'s bobblehead of a football quarterback, Kevin. I discovered a newfound appreciation for (ugh, yes, too long) basketball shorts by enjoying the charms of one Fresh Prince of Bel-Air. I swooned over *Buffy*'s Xander in a Speedo and the titular lead of *Dawson's Creek* in a towel. Heck, even the glimpses of Urkel's—er, I'm sorry, Stefan's—chiseled torso, were enough to pique my interest and lay bare (pun intended) the bodies my schoolmates kept to themselves at school. But none, perhaps, caught my eye quite like the all-star jock of Bayside High, *Saved by the Bell*'s A.C. Slater. The reason? The many sights we got of actor Mario Lopez strutting around in nothing more than a wrestling singlet.

As any red-blooded gay teen whose eyes constantly scanned my surroundings for any hints of the naked male body—everything from underwear ads to tight-fitting uniform pants—Slater was a revelation. As was his signature scarlet singlet, a piece of clothing that was as revealing as it was demure. Given that our school barely gave any thought to sports outside of soccer, wrestling was a foreign concept to me. As was any kind of sport where one's body was so displayed. And the singlet, a sporting piece of clothing that's designed to showcase the male body at its most elemental—as a chiseled weapon ready to strike—was, put simply, awe-inspiring. Not for nothing did *The New York Times*—in a piece about the suggestive nature of this traditional wrestling garment—describe the singlet as "basically an oversize jock-strap with suspenders," adding that "if the uniforms are considered unappealing for what they may reveal, well, that is part of the allure for wrestling enthusiasts who consider the sport to be the ultimate test of manhood." Therein lay its allure. The image of the wrestler, even one as charming and unassuming as that of Slater, can't help but conjure up both aggression and eroticism; the male body so revealed is both a come-on and a threat. It is manhood distilled.

It's no surprise the wrestling body opens up questions of what a seemingly self-evident concept like "manhood" is all about. You need only look at films like *Foxcatcher* (where Channing Tatum all but bulges out of his singlet amid a story about fragile egos and bruised male friendships) and novels like *Stephen Florida* (where Gabe Habash's titular hero unravels after an injury derails his college wrestling plans) and *In One Person* (where the wrestling body becomes, quite literally, a clue to a genderqueer mystery in John Irving's coming-of-age tale) to notice the thematic richness of such a sport when it comes to young men's vexed and vexing relationships with their own bodies. Before them all—to my eyes, at least—was Slater, who became an avatar for many a high school athlete who wrestled with what it meant to be a man, all while becoming, in turn, a swoon-worthy crush for many of us who wrestled, instead, with what it meant to want one.

In *Saved by the Bell*'s very first episode, Slater arrives at The Max diner in his singlet and a pair of gray sweatpants, armed with an over-sized wrestling trophy in hand. His athletic prowess, and his ability to steal the spotlight from Mark-Paul Gosselaar's Zack Morris (who'd been bragging about his third-place finish in a far less interesting competition) immediately set him up as the blond teen's foil. In fact, this episode revolves around Zack's insecurity over Slater's dance moves, which he fears might be electrifying enough to woo young Kelly (Tiffani-Amber Thiessen) away from him. Slater's command of his body, on the mat and on the dance floor, structures the way both Zack and the show understand him; his allure is tied to the aggression and eroticism his body exudes.

Producer Peter Engel, who'd retooled the Disney Channel sitcom *Good Morning, Miss Bliss* (1987–1989) into the NBC show that would go on to make Zack Morris and his crew household names, had wanted to give his cheeky protagonist a rival of sorts. Enter Slater, a character that was originally conceived as a John Travolta type. He was to be an Italian American student whose swagger would play off Morris's more sardonic demeanor. It was only after failing to find an appropriate Italian American actor that casting broadened its search, making way for Lopez. The young Mexican American actor was an accomplished amateur wrestler, as well as a break-dancer and drummer, elements that would further define Slater over the next five years (and in a later reboot of the series). That meant the young actor's body was central to how the character was (re)imagined for the screen; Lopez's athletic prowess made Slater a magnetic presence, equally equipped to seduce as to threaten.

I don't know when or how I first started watching *Saved by the Bell*. We didn't have NBC in Colombia, of course. And from what I gather, the Disney Channel (which our satellite dish provider *did* include and which introduced me to such shows as *Adventures in Wonderland, Under the Umbrella Tree*, and *Adventures of the Gummi Bears*) only ever aired *Good Morning, Miss Bliss*. Given the success of the retooled show, I'm convinced I must have caught not its original run (I was only five years old when its first season aired on NBC) but some syndicated reruns years thereafter. In any case, I vividly remember watching Zack con his friends or principal Belding or some other unsuspecting mark into one harebrained scheme or another. I recall many iconic "very special episodes"—particularly the one about Jessie (Elizabeth Berkley) struggling with caffeine pills that has since spawned a million memes—as well as its many sequels, which followed the Bayside kids to college, to Hawaii, and even to Vegas for its final wedding-themed TV-movie. That I can't place where I first watched it speaks, perhaps, to my rabid consumption of U.S. media growing up. There was always something incredibly alluring about watching these imported shows—especially those about kids and teens my age. Mostly because they were so foreign to my own experience.

Much is made of the way television brings characters into our homes. Taking up space in our living rooms, it's as if they were (or could be) part of our family. That wasn't the case at our house: TV sets belonged in bedrooms, never in public spaces. Shared viewing experiences did not take place on couches squarely positioned in front of the TV; our living room, in fact, always felt oppressively decorative, with oversized leather sofas crowding the space, furniture once bought for a larger apartment before my mother had to downsize following her divorce. Instead, family screenings took place in my mom's bedroom, all three of her kids cozied up under blankets in her king-sized bed. Or on weekends, when we were whisked off to her office as she caught up on work, in a conference room where fights over the remote eventually led to very civil one-hour shifts that kept my little brother, my sister, and me shuttling from Nickelodeon toons to MTV countdowns to nineties sitcoms on any given Saturday. And every night, much to my brother's chagrin, it was I who controlled our bedroom's comically small TV set.

These characters I let into my bedroom spurred many a teenage realization about who I was, who I could be, and who I would want (to be). In many ways, television structured my days. Movies may have been an escape, a weekend treat that let me think back to once upon a time or let me travel to galaxies far, far away. But television was home. TV shows were digestible windows into plausible lives lived next door—even when they took place miles and miles away. Moreover, shows like *Saved by the Bell*, no matter how contrived and inauthentic they were, allowed me a glimpse into that most mythical of spaces: the all-American high school. Here's where I should explain a bit about the collegiate environment I grew up in and give you a sense of why the concept of "high school" didn't register in my vocabulary. When I was four years old, my mother enrolled me in a British private school in Bogotá that prided itself on its bilingual education and its ties to the United Kingdom. As with most private schools in Bogotá, my school welcomed kids at age four for their kindergarten years and followed them for close to fifteen years through primary and later secondary school. The classmates I met when I was a precocious four-year-old were the same ones I graduated with when I was a sullen, nerdy eighteen-year-old.

On-screen, U.S. kids worried about the move from middle school to high school. There was, so I learned, a nerve-wracking shift that occurred then: there'd be a whole new school to navigate and old friends to mourn, new friends to make and old habits to break. Not so in my case. Yes, you slowly got to explore more and more of the grounds of the school—including the grassy annexed lot that felt ready-made to give teenagers a sense of unbridled privacy away from school buildings and teachers. And you got to spend more hours on the premises as you grew up (kindergarteners went home at noon, before lunch, while primary students stayed until 2:30 p.m.; secondary students an extra hour past that). But for all intents and purposes, there was familiarity and a sense of permanence. Moreover, *secondary school* (*bachillerato*) didn't really have the same ring to it as *high school*. There was the obsequious Britishness of it all, for starters. With our blue ties and blazers, we all looked more like something out of a boarding school in England than the dizzying and colorful world of an all-American high school. It's why we all cherished the few "Jeans Days" we got each year. Watching students navigate Bayside High felt like an opportunity to witness a different world entirely. A world where every day was Jeans Day.

If I'm stuck on our uniforms, it's because they were my first lesson in gendered self-expression. While boys and girls alike were required to wear pristine white shirts along with our ties and sweaters, for the majority of my time at school, girls were also required to wear pleated skirts—and tights underneath them, of course. Their length was a constant source of tension between teachers and students; many of my classmates would fold their waistbands several times during recess to hike up their skirts, only to be reprimanded once they returned to class. In a space where we all wore the same thing, with only minor size alterations (a baggy sweater here, a too-tight pair of pants there), skirts were the most obvious way boys and girls were set apart. There was no escaping that this kind of dress code was more about controlling girls' self-presentation than anything remotely pedagogical. Never, in the conversations parents and students alike had about the potential of allowing girls to wear pants, was there any discussion about boys' bodies or boys' dress codes. As is so often the case, men's bodies afforded themselves a kind of privileged invisibility; you didn't ever need to think about them.

Back then I also didn't need to look far to find probing takes on gender presentation—or handy examples of what young male bodies could mean. I only needed to turn on the TV and visit Bayside High. Throughout its four-year run, *Saved by the Bell* made Slater's jock body and Zack's attendant anxieties twinned problems that distilled ongoing cultural conversations about changing gender relations in the United States, many of which felt familiar enough to a young Colombian teen who saw in both boys different ways of being a young man in the nineties. This was never more obvious than in the many episodes that centered on Slater's wrestling prowess. Take the aptly titled episode "Pinned to the Mat," from the show's freshman season. It's career week at Bayside and our teen protagonists are urged to think about their future. Their career goals, as we soon learn, stay true to their archetypal molds: fashionista Lisa Turtle (Lark Vorhies) hopes to become a designer; socially conscious Jessie is set on becoming a judge; true to his geeky predilections, Screech (Dustin Diamond) has dreams of being an astronaut; ever the traditionalist, Kelly wants nothing more than to be a mom and a housewife; while vain and needy Zack can't imagine himself doing anything other than hosting a game show. It's only Slater who stumbles when projecting his teenage self into the future. When prodded, he offers as simple an answer as he can muster: "I'll be a wrestler!"

Slater's tunnel vision about his future earns him the scorn of his friends. They egg him on to imagine a time when he won't be able to rely on his toned, teenage body for success, a point the show furthers with a fantasy sequence set years into the future where Slater, now a leopard-print-wearing, beer-bellied pro wrestler, is the laughingstock of Bayside's alumni reunion. This nightmarish scenario pushes the young athlete to rethink his high school ambitions. Zack, ever the trickster, cons Slater into *not* quitting wrestling (there's a bet on an upcoming match Zack can't afford to lose). In a roundabout move, Zack suggests Slater try joining the cooking club, a place he promises will be filled with girls he can flirt with. His ulterior motive is quickly spelled out in one of Zack's signature fourth-wall-breaking moments: "Slater in an apron? He'll be laughed right back into the gym!"

This line of comedy feels all too familiar. Domesticity, the show proudly implied, is the stuff of girls, not the stuff of men. And definitely not the stuff of men like Slater. Such quaint fodder for comedy sounds (or should sound) hilariously outdated. This wasn't just an obvious punchline back then. It was an unavoidable comedic setup in the late eighties and early nineties; the mere thought of men embracing caretaking tasks was the stuff of broad, mainstream comedy. There was *Mr. Mom* (1983) finding the humor in a clueless out-of-work engineer needing to stay at home and take care of the kids while his wife went back into the workforce. There was *Three Men and a Baby* (1987) wringing laughs out of three bachelors at a loss as to how to care for a baby girl. There was *Look Who's Talking* (1989) turning a roughened cab driver into a beloved nanny amid a playful romantic comedy.

Even the plot of the uproariously funny *Mrs. Doubtfire* (1993), about a divorced man who impersonates an elderly female nanny to grow closer to his kids, relied on the way Robin Williams's Daniel Hillard was ill-equipped to live by himself, let alone take care of his three kids.

The image of the hapless man learning the hard way what it's like to take on the role of caretaker found its most lauded example not in a laugh-out-loud comedy but in one of the most tear-jerking dramas of the late twentieth century. The Oscar-winning *Kramer vs. Kramer* (1979) may have been structured around a bitter divorce between Meryl Streep's Joanna and Dustin Hoffman's Ted, but its most poignant moments came courtesy of the scenes where Ted, left to raise his young boy by himself, has to adapt to being a single working parent. On the first morning Ted is alone with his eight-year-old kid, for instance, he tries to play off his haplessness for humor; he promises young Billy French toast but soon realizes such a simple breakfast menu item is out of his wheelhouse. He gets broken egg shells on the eggs (all while pointing out that all chefs are men, did Billy know that?) and is flummoxed when he finds there's no easy way of dipping a slice of bread into the mug he's been using to whip said eggs ("Uh, we fold it!" he bluffs, before Billy protests that he doesn't like his bread in pieces). He then forgets to add milk to the French toast mix, botches making coffee in his French press, and burns his hand when trying to keep the soggy, egg-soaked fiasco from activating the kitchen smoke detector—all before dropping everything on the floor, cursing his situation ("Goddamnit!") and his defecting wife ("God damn her!"). It is all, in a word, a mess.

Kramer vs. Kramer's Hoffman was—like *Three Men and a Baby*'s Tom Selleck and Ted Danson, and *Look Who's Talking*'s John Travolta—an icon of a modern American masculinity. For a generation who'd grown up on *The Graduate*, where Hoffman had flaunted the very rules of bourgeois respectability, who'd rooted for Selleck's gruff Magnum, P.I., who'd come to know and love Danson's womanizing

Sam Malone in *Cheers*, and who'd seen Travolta strut his way through New York City in *Saturday Night Fever*, these men represented welcome variations of what a "man" could be; they were iconoclasts in their own way. Watching them navigate the perils of housework and fatherhood was what made their respective star vehicles so intriguing, alluring even. That these Hollywood hits were springing up in tandem with a slew of films about women's empowered roles in the workplace (think *9 to 5*, *Baby Boom*, and *Working Girls*, to name but a few) was not coincidental. Hollywood comedies had never been shy about mining the differences between the sexes for humor (screwball comedy all but depends on it), but there was a streak of darkened melancholy that undergirded these new attempts to laugh at the way men and women were being called to rethink their own roles in society.

That such conversations would trickle down to the treacly trappings of shows like *Saved by the Bell* isn't surprising. But revisiting this childhood favorite, armed with decades of gender and queer theory in my head, makes those many wrestling storylines like the cooking club one—where Slater at first excels at baking a delicious cake but is eventually wooed back to the mat when he's called to play hero and save scrawny Screech from getting his ass beat—feel like missed opportunities for the show to have dug into anxieties about an increasingly fractured view of gender roles in the 1990s. These plotlines were junior-sized versions of those big-screen comedies. When lines like, "Think you're man enough for cooking club?" made in-person audiences guffaw and plots about the absurd prospect of female wrestlers had viewers in stitches, it's easy to see why Slater was the perfect vehicle through which to funnel these anxieties. A tough guy on the outside who paraded his biceps and pectorals with gleeful pride in tight-fitting singlets, Slater was a character who was constantly asked to soften himself, to make himself be more vulnerable—to reveal himself emotionally as easily and as seductively as he did so physically.

In one famous sequence, he sets out to woo Jessie after refusing to attend the ballet with her (he'd rather they have spent their evening at a football game) by staging a makeshift ballet performance for her, wearing a black bodysuit that was as revealing as those singlets he usually donned. With hoots and hollers from the live studio audience (who clearly reveled in watching Lopez do what was ostensibly a stripper tear-away reveal), here was yet another instance where gendered roles and expectations were blurred in Slater's own body. In that single image, Slater (and Lopez, in turn) captured what could potentially be the premise to a homophobic callout (look! an athlete dancing ballet!) as well as a homoerotic pinup (look! a hunk in tights!), yet he dances around them with aplomb. Slater's jock-like exterior was always running up against these softer—and, for many characters, contentious—preferences, storylines, and anxieties that literalized the question the singlet has come to stand for: How much of the male body can be revealed (can be made vulnerable) before it spills over into indecent, or sexual, or yes, homoerotic, if not outright gay, territory?

Collier Schorr's photo series on high school wrestlers began as an exploration into that very space where she had glimpsed a broader concept of masculinity than what is ordinarily captured in American culture, high and low alike. "I can only approach it as a woman," she explained in 2003, "but—for me, from the outside, masculinity has been depicted in very black and white terms. There never seems to be a wide range of emotional definitions of men." On the wrestling mat, and particularly during practice, she'd come to see how aggression and tenderness could coexist. Whenever she'd grab her camera to document these meets, she'd be most taken by instances where two teammates would throw moves together only to pull themselves apart and make sure they hadn't hurt one another. It was in those moments of twinship and opposition—which very much describe this most performatively violent of sports—that Schorr saw her project truly come together. Any one of the many portraits she's taken of wrestlers over the years—some in repose, some mid-fight, some bathed in glory, some awash in defeat—offers a fascinating snapshot into this young man's world. Under the glare of her flash, these athletes alternate between being on display and being seen; the former seems to be their initial instinct when faced with a camera, the latter the result.

No photo exemplifies this as well as "Momentarily Out of Place (H.T. & A.M.)." In the 2002 picture, two shirtless young men are standing against a darkened background, seen from their torsos up. Their skin is aglow with sweat. Their nipples are perked and pointed. Only a smattering of chest and facial hair adorn their otherwise smooth bodies. The one on the left, his dark hair in a prim and proper buzz cut, eyes clocked on our gaze, is leaning on his fellow wrestler, whose gaze is cast down. There's a youthfulness to the boy who caught Schorr's eyes, his plump red lips and his hardened jawline working in tandem with his defined pecs and abs to evoke the unintended eroticism the photographer has long insisted her subjects exude but which she never aims to excavate. But there is something seductive about pose and frame alike, especially if you know that right off frame were two other wrestlers, posing with their singlets rolled down to their waists. Unlike the photos Schorr has taken and displayed of wrestlers on the mat or pinned to the floor, "Momentarily Out of Place (H.T. & A.M.)," as its title suggests, finds these high schoolers away from their element, out of sync even, with their intended goal when sporting the singlet. Their camaraderie, which is so central to the sport (even in practice you can't wrestle alone), is captured at its most fleeting (for even in practice, only one can prevail).

When presented with such imagery, as Schorr herself is aware, many of us will fixate on what we know, looking to align a photo like "Momentarily Out of Place (H.T. & A.M.)" with similar content. I can't speak for others, but in my case, a moment like the one captured by Schorr is enough to titillate me for the sheer closeness it depends on. Athletics are one of the few socially sanctioned spheres where men's bodies and homosocial bonding are both encouraged and publicized. Seeing two sweat-tinged bodies so casually intertwined is, in my head, only a heartbeat away from something delightfully more not-safe-for-work. This is, perhaps, why singlets and equally sugges- tive athletic gear so pervade the realm of gay porn. To think of those tightly pumped bodies engaging in a decidedly more lascivious scene is pure fantasy, yes. One that, at its core, tries to rewire the markers of masculine ideals as inherently homoerotic: those bulging biceps aren't for punching but for caressing (or, in some cases, for consensual choking); those tight asses aren't mere by-products of arduous train- ing but open invitations (in ways more literal than you can imagine). This isn't anything new. The line between aggressive heterosexuality and rampant homoeroticism has long been a porous one. Already in the 1960s—with the rise in popularity of beefcake photography and magazines such as *Physique Pictorial*—anxieties over the associations between homosexuality and bodybuilding, for instance, had led both *Sports Illustrated* and *The New York Times* to decry the way so-called wholesome activities like weight lifting had been overrun by a "lu- natic fringe." As David K. Johnson puts it in his book *Buying Gay: How Physique Entrepreneurs Sparked a Movement*, "Family physicians were known to warn teenage boys away from lifting weights because of the likelihood of encountering homosexuals." In the decades since such mid-century anxieties made national headlines and, as Johnson chronicles, constituted the central arguments of many an obscenity trial, the (homo)eroticization of the athletic male body has continued apace, with wrestlers in particular standing in as obvious targets for such lustful gazing.

When I think back to the breathless moralizing that Johnson cites, it makes me value the ubiquity with which I see such gazing on beautifully toned bodies. I need only go on Instagram, for instance, and find many an account whose sole purpose is to provide me with the kind of content that would've been deemed illegal at worst and amoral at best back in the 1950s and '60s when photographers like

Bob Mizer were (re)claiming the male body as an erotic object worthy of our attention. Mizer's photos of scantily clad young, athletic men in pinup poses formed the backbone of the famed and infamous *Physique Pictorial* quarterly magazine, whose publishing history from 1951 to 1990 pioneered a new wave of publications aimed at gay men that includes local magazines like Toronto's *TWO* (1964), Philadelphia's *Drum* (1964), and New York City's *Christopher Street* (1976) as well as national ones like *The Advocate* (1967). Mizer's models (often hustlers, sailors, and even former inmates) fit into the fantasies of masculine ideals the photographer so enjoyed (re)creating with his images, which freely played with Greco-Roman archetypes as well as well-worn fetishistic scenarios (namely lots of wrestlers and jocks). His influence can be felt in everything from Robert Mapplethorpe's nude photography to David Hockney's sensory paintings. Indeed, such an aesthetic was gaining ground in the latter half of the twentieth century. Already in the 1970s, Andrew Holleran, perhaps best known as a chronicler of New York City with his classic novel *Dancer from the Dance*, made clear the way this brand of athletic masculinity had taken over the urbane gay male scene in the city. In an essay titled "Male Nudes and Nude Males," Holleran bemoaned the uniformity of the bodies he'd encounter. A friend had even confided in him how, after joining a gym downtown, he'd gotten a personal trainer to agree to give him a chest, broad shoulders, and a V shape ("it was just like shopping at Saks," the friend quipped). Before, the beautiful bodies were few and far between; they were events. But that was changing: "people wear bodies now the way they wore plaid shirts four years ago," Holleran writes. "And if a body is something people can just put on—the way we chose our favorite plaid—then isn't it just one more accoutrement?" Holleran was unexpectedly diagnosing a shift in how gay men approached their own bodies—no doubt anticipating the arrival of what Mark Simpson dubs the modern "spornosexual," portmanteauing *sport* and *porn* as characteristic of the 0 percent body fat yet muscled men of the twenty-first century. Imagery of athletic prowess was repurposed and appropriated as signaling (and demanding, really) queer desire. Holleran's complaints and Simpson's apt moniker no doubt gave way to the parade of images that now populate our social media feeds.

For a twenty-first-century audience, the notion of indulging in such homoerotic portraiture may feel if not quaint then not nearly as radical as it did when Mizer and his ilk had to fight draconian decency laws to let their work be widely distributed. But a newer generation of artists is continually reframing how it is we can think about and look at male bodies, in ever more creative ways. And many of them are doing so on platforms that are outright hostile to such endeavors. Take Portis Wasp, a mixed media artist who makes digital still and moving image collages. His work, which he posts on Instagram (an online space that continues to shadow ban and delete queer artists' profiles), blends editorial photographs with, say, screenshots from films: a *Call Me by Your Name* still intercut with photos of Orlando Bloom from an *Esquire* shoot; a Jake Gyllenhaal *Style* cover image where the actor's pink sweatered torso is replaced with a pair of imposing, hairy pecs. One of his most intriguing ongoing series is titled "Adidass." Just as his cheeky collages poke fun and mine the homoerotic in our contemporary image culture, this sporadic series literally rebrands photographs of athletes to draw attention to their awe-inspiring rear ends. Adding that one extra *s* to the athletic brand's logo, Wasp reminds us just how much the frame put around an image can alter not only its intended audience but its latent meaning. For instance, the image of two wrestlers hugging one another, captured in profile (an angle that very much accentuates their asses) is stripped of the sportsmanship it was capturing and is, instead, intentionally reframed as an intimately erotic portrait. It's not just reframed still photography. Followers of @portiswasp1 (the added number denoting that his content has already once been deemed too salacious for the increasingly prudish standards Meta, Instagram's parent company, enforces) are sometimes treated to three- to four-second videos where we see wrestlers walking away from the mat, or hydrating with the help of their coaches. There's subversion here, but also an entrenchment of masculine ideals. Another way to think about it is that this is but the latest iteration of a long lineage of gay male art-making wherein athletic masculinity becomes but another fetish.

Not for nothing did Hal Fischer, in his seminal 1970s *Gay Semiotics* photography project, include a "Street Fashion Jock." In the picture, taken out in the street, a young bearded man is seen leisurely slouching against a concrete wall. His rugged appearance (he has a well-kept beard and shaggy but nicely combed parted hair) makes his sporty outfit all the more remarkable, especially given how skinny he appears with one of his lanky arms resting softly on the one leg pushing him away from the wall behind him. The clothing is precisely what Fischer was most interested in. As he helpfully identifies with typed labels overlaid on the black-and-white photo, the young man is wearing a "sleeveless undershirt" that frames his lithe frame, "satin gym shorts" that leave little to the imagination, and "white socks," as well as, yes, a pair of Adidas. Creating his project as a way to index urban gay male culture, Fischer hoped to chronicle the way gay men were using markers (handkerchiefs, keys, earrings, but also athletic and leather gear, and even cowboy garments) to communicate sexual preference. In his words, "a sexual semiotic was developed." Not just developed, but resignified. After all, it took a specific kind of gaze to realize that the combination of Adidas shoes and satin gym shorts had less to do with a guy's athleticism than with his sexual proclivities.

Schorr's work can't help but be in conversation with that semiotic, particularly because she captures its imagery in a space seemingly divorced from the context Fischer articulates. "Momentarily Out of Place (H.T. & A.M.)" rubs right up against that gay aesthetic, yet the photographer's work almost begs us to uncouple such homoeroticism from its frame. There are dueling instincts here: to only ever understand such candid (and near-naked) vulnerability as intrinsically erotic is to deprive young men (regardless of their sexuality) of a kind of bonding and a kind of openness that needs to be nurtured. But to explicitly deny the sexual pull such images can have, and to frame them (as *Sports Illustrated* did back in the 1960s and many a "no homo" bro has since) as inviolate and immune to such gazes is to feed into a toxicity that refuses to let men be unwittingly desired (by other men). This is why the image of the young wrestler in (just) his singlet feels so rife for deconstruction: a body sculpted for fighting has become a fetishistic sexual fantasy. It sits at the intersection of what we demand socially of certain young boys and what we chastise in certain others. But there's no denying such a semiotic was in constant conversation with the uplifted ideal of masculinity it imitated. If athletic masculinity has become a fetish, a body to be donned just as easily as, say, a fashionable plaid shirt, how has it reframed the bonds and gazes it nurtures in its wake?

In thinking of this conundrum, I'm left to wonder how much of what I find sexy about these young athletes in repose is rooted in my exaltation of a masculinity I cannot myself inhabit. The Lacanian in me can't escape the thought that what I desire is that which I lack, a formulation whose simplicity makes it all the more appealing. But it can't quite capture what happens in those moments when a flexed bicep or a toned ass causes more than a mere swoon, especially when framed by a tight-fitting singlet. For, if I wanted, I could very well pump my own muscles at the gym (which I do) and don such a singlet (which I have done). But there's a hollowness to that image of me in the mirror. I am no athlete. I'm definitely no wrestler. And so what I lack and what I desire is not the image of the wrestler as much as what he represents. Aggression, for one. And heterosexuality, no doubt. But also a welcome submission, to my gaze, to my own lust. Is that then a subversion of the patriarchal masculinity I've grown and been groomed to admire, fear, and aspire to? Or is it merely a capitulation to its hold on my sexual imagination?

This goes beyond those Instagram accounts I follow. I think back to the seminal (pun intended) gay porn that flourished in the early 2000s when a mere click transported me to endless nondescript living rooms and bedrooms where young, muscled hunks allowed themselves (or so they told us) to be touched for the very first time by friends or roommates or fellow gym buds. Gay porn studios like Bel Ami, Sean Cody, CockyBoys, Corbin Fisher, and the like fed into these fantasies with winking spunk (pun intended), creating modern riffs on gay-for-pay porn and continuing the history of hardcore videos as enshrining a very specific brand of coveted bodies. As gay porn historian Jeffrey Escoffier explains, "gay hardcore also reinforced the new style of gay masculinity—it recorded (almost like a 'documentary') and codified the new masculine sexual ethos that was emerging among gay men. Gay porn, as a genre," he continues, "portrayed 'straight' men engaging in homosexual acts. It thus served to situate homosexual *desire* within masculine territory irrespective of heterosexual or gay identities." There's an expansiveness to this formulation. But also a narrow view of what that "masculine territory" can and does look like: not all men have toned muscles nor do they all need to (or do) value the strength and virility they clearly stand in for.

Yet for those of us who seek out porn that, for instance, features drunken bros playing beer pong in a Michigan dorm before turning into a debaucherous and lecherous good time among naked friends (where one guy's imposing chest is accentuated by the sweat-tinged body paint he's got on), there's plenty to examine in how we may be glamorizing men who could easily turn us into punchlines if not outright into punching bags. It's a double-edged sword of a lesson on the aesthetics of masculinity I wrestle with every time I put on (or merely admire) a singlet. The conviction that maybe we could prize it if only we could prise it out of the hands of those who'd wield it against us is as alluring as it is illusory. But not for that any less enticing.

3.

Hombres

THE WORD *TELENOVELA* HAS LONG FASCINATED ME. UNLIKE
the sudsy connotations of its English-language analogue (*soap opera*),
there is no inherent, if playful, linguistic put-down in the expression
itself. Nor such an immediate association with its profit-driven enter-
prise. Rather than finding their genre lexically attached to soap companies and radio serials, telenovelas suggest instead quite a cultured
pedigree: they are, if we take them literally, televised novels. Such a
combination, fittingly marrying high and low culture in the blink of
a syllable, is what so appeals to me.

Not coincidentally, my introduction to telenovelas was tied to
my own literary education. During the years when I was reading the
works of Gabriel García Márquez, Juan Rulfo, Carlos Fuentes, and
Julio Cortázar in Spanish class and John Steinbeck, Margaret At-
wood, and Tennessee Williams in English class, my evenings were
spent enjoying the latest productions from Televisa, TV Azteca, RTI,
Caracol, and RCN—prolific companies whose telenovelas dominated
Mexican and Colombian prime time. The simultaneous discovery of
novelas and telenovelas meant they were always intertwined in my
imagination. Just as they are, as it turns out, intertwined in their
own respective twentieth-century histories: Colombian producers

had initially mined literary texts for inspiration, adapting classics like Jorge Isaacs's *María* (aired in 1972 and later remade in 1991 with a script by García Márquez), Mario Vargas Llosa's *La tía Julia y el escribidor* (1981), and even Rulfo's *El gallo de oro* (1982) to great acclaim. The novels that made Colombia and Latin America the toast of the global literary world following the so-called boom (best encapsulated by García Márquez's 1982 Nobel Prize) and the telenovelas that delighted television viewers all over the continent in the late twentieth century suggest a kinship between them that may not feel immediately apparent.

In a 1988 interview aptly headlined "Las telenovelas son una maravilla" ("Telenovelas are a wonder"), the Nobel Prize winner scolded those who looked down on television's growing cultural importance. "Lo que pasa es que ya tenemos un condicionamiento mental que nos hace pensar que una telenovela es sinónimo de cursi, pero yo no lo creo así." What's happened, he argued then, was that we'd been conditioned to think that a telenovela was synonymous with something *cursi*, but that needn't and shouldn't be the case. Like much regionally specific slang, *cursi* demands I mistranslate it as I try to convey what it connotes. First off, you should always read it with a sneer on your face. You never want to come off as cursi. You should be ashamed if anything you do is so described. It's not just earnestness, though there is that. And it's not quite sentimental, though that's part of it too. The word is not ever solely used as a put-down descriptor of performative emotional outbursts, but one thing is always clear: it is rarely used as a positive quality. For there's a treacly sweetness to something *cursi*, like a giant teddy bear as a gift on Valentine's Day or a mariachi serenade outside your window, gestures that make some blush with appreciation and others with secondhand embarrassment. But there's also an inherent condescension in dubbing something *cursi*, as if all our romantic narrative templates were too simple and simplified. The fact that such a word also carries with it a whiff of the elitism that remains rampant in Colombia merely reinforces the notion that unabashed melodrama is the stuff of the masses, an argument that's as old as the genre itself.

García Márquez's own plots pilfered freely from the realm of the *cursi*. He's long credited those outsized melodramas his grandmother so giddily regaled him with in his youth as being central not only to his narratives but also to his own storytelling sensibility. The author understood that there was something of value therein, that such maudlin sentimentality could be the source of great cultural impact. This is why, for him, telenovelas captured a kind of education on what was craved and what was to be coveted. They helped structure how we understand ourselves and gave us templates for how to love. They even offered us visions of what to aspire to, which could be as limiting as they could be expansive. My mom, who preferred the lavish, ensemble-driven telenovelas that came out of Brazil (her favorite was an Agatha Christie–like whodunit aptly titled *La próxima víctima*, which had more gore than romance), would never dare admit how much this genre infiltrated our family's own sentimental education.

Our family history, as she always put it, was more the stuff of García Márquez novels, intricately woven tales that defied belief. She loved egging on my grandmother, a consummate storyteller from the coast who knew how to wring a laugh out of a rapt audience of one, to share the more outlandish stories that had been told so many times they'd ossified into their own magically real tales. Did I know that Alcoholics Anonymous had first arrived in Colombia because of one of our relatives, who used to get so drunk he built himself a cage so his family could lock him up whenever he went on one of his benders? Was I aware that my grandmother's sister had the gift of premonition, at times seeing in dreams which family member would soon pass? Had I heard about the time my great-grandfather, visiting New York City decades after going to school there, had come face-to-face with the son he never knew he had—randomly at a bar, no less? Even the bits of family lore that didn't obviously rub up against national history, the supernatural, or the uproariously implausible, felt taken out of the pages of a thrilling epic story. Some stories reached back all the way to Spain and Portugal, where a distant Jewish ancestor had, with his family, fled persecution only to marry a nice Catholic girl once he reached the Americas. Others felt like psychological horror tales, like the one about the cousin several times removed whose wife killed herself just as his own mother had when he was a kid, or the one about my great-grandmother who went mad after getting knocked off a horse. I must admit, even my grandmother's courtship—which began with meeting my grandfather at a wedding and continued in letters written back and forth between her native Barranquilla near the north coast and my grandfather's home in the high Andean mountains of Medellín—had the ring of García Márquez's best-selling novel *El amor en los tiempos del cólera*, based as it was on his own parents' love story. Which is all to say: the romance of melodramas was inescapable even in my family's own self-made myths.

Then again, my mother has never been one for sweeping romantic dramas. She may love *Gone with the Wind*, but in her telling, that's a book (and film) about a woman's resilience. She rarely talks about Rhett Butler. She opts instead to drive home those final Scarlett O'Hara lines about tomorrow being another day. So well-worn was this cribbed mantra that whenever she uttered it, in hopes of comforting us about a bad grade or an awful fight with a friend, it earned an eye roll from all three of us kids. Similarly, though she was often transfixed by Brazilian telenovelas, she'd always talk about the period costumes before ever mentioning the central love story. I wouldn't go so far as to say she was a cynic when it came to romance, but her pop culture tastes fell distinctly outside the realm of melodrama. As a kid, and later as a teen, I thought this had to do with her worldly sensibility. This was a young woman who grew up obsessed with The Beatles and Queen, who was won over by Harrison Ford's Han Solo

and Indiana Jones, and who would later go on to swoon over George
Clooney in *E.R.* To this day, and even after decades of living with
and working alongside her boyfriend, she has no rosy aspirations to
remarry nor to live out the kind of happily ever after our extended
family members so extol.

I don't know whether her acrimonious divorce from my father,
which left her stranded in Bogotá away from family in Medellín with
no money and three young kids to raise by herself, soured her outlook
on the prescriptive notions of marriage and family that so surrounded
us. What I do know is that, unlike my grandmother and my aunts—
all of whom badgered my sister even in her teens about making sure
she was on the hunt for the right boy to marry, and who placed undue
value on throwing lavish wedding parties, finding a stable job, and
raising a house full of kids as markers of success—my mom always
encouraged all three of us to instead follow our own paths. Romance
wasn't ever the story for her; love was a narrative she didn't put much
stock in. It wasn't just telenovelas that she balked at; she had no time
for rom-coms, chick flicks, or any kind of maudlin melodrama. There
was no time for such *cursilería*.

That may be why telenovelas so enthralled me. As a child of divorce, I had to seek in popular culture the love stories that felt so sul-
lied around me in real life. And (it seems so reductive; it would only
get thornier as I got older) I sought male role models in them because
they were so absent at home. And reader, what I ran up against was
nothing short of disheartening. Mostly because what I saw on-screen
often felt like outsized examples of the claustrophobic ideals I was
running away from in my own life. As a genre, the Latin American
telenovela hinged always (even in those targeted at younger crowds)
on romance: boy meets girl, boy eventually marries girl. Yes, a bunch
of stuff usually happened in between those two plot points, but the
endings would almost always be the same, and no matter where the
story was set, monogamous heterosexual love was exalted above all

else. And yet, even when no one remotely like me (not just queer, but bookish and shy, nerdy and sarcastic) was at the center of these stories, there was comfort in losing myself in a predictable storyline where go-getting women would always be rewarded with the handsomest (and often the richest) of men. They were never aspirational in my eyes—I knew they were a fanciful fantasy packaged to amuse us every day—but they were what I looked forward to on any given night.

Even at age eleven, I knew *Hombres* was a decidedly modern provocation. The title alone set it apart from many of the telenovelas being produced both at home and abroad. Men were rarely front and center in this genre of prime-time television. There were leading men in dramas like *Eternamente Manuela*, *María la del barrio*, *La potra Zaina*, and *La mujer doble*, of course. But the melodramatic trappings of shows with names like *Ruta del destino*, *Pasiones secretas*, *El último beso*, *Lazos de amor*, and *Prisionera de amor* were anchored by their captivating heroines, young women who had to fend off a world that worked to deny them their happily ever after for hundreds of episodes on end. That changed with this new project by then-up-and-coming telenovela writer and showrunner Mónica Agudelo.

When *Hombres*'s first episode aired on Canal A in 1996, Colombian telenovelas were at the brink of a global explosion. *Café con aroma de mujer* (1994–1995), which starred Guy Ecker and Margarita Rosa de Francisco, had become an unlikely hit that crossed borders and found a massive global audience. Set against one of Colombia's most well-known exporting industries—his family owns a coffee business; she harvests coffee beans on his family's hacienda— *Café* wasn't just a ratings hit at home, it was a phenomenon. Roughly three out of every four television sets tuned in nightly to see whether the wily Gaviota (de Francisco) and the dashing Sebastián (Ecker) would overcome their differences (and his snobbish family) to live out the shared life they both dreamed of. The show, which has been remade in Mexico twice over and again in Colombia in 2021, was an international hit as well as a powerful calling card for the Colombian television industry, which has only grown in esteem in the decades since.

The success of Colombian telenovelas is best encapsulated by the mammoth success of *Yo soy Betty, la fea* (1999–2001), which would go on to inspire ABC's *Ugly Betty* (2006–2010) in the States and spawn over twenty remakes around the world, earning in the process a Guinness World Record citation for most successful telenovela of all time. Like *Café*, *Betty* was an RCN production that used a celebrated Colombian industry, in this case fashion, to anchor an age-old romantic drama, here between a dowdy, bespectacled nerd and a rakish hunk of an executive.

Just as I'd found a wealth of complex, fascinating women in lavish animated musicals during the so-called Disney renaissance, telenovelas like *Café* and *Betty* had plenty of alluring female protagonists. Indeed, these narratives often depended on their heroines suffering needlessly but coming out on top; De Francisco's Gaviota and Ana María Orozco's Betty are assertive, self-made women who, even if blindly driven by love for a man, become astute career women who are able to support their families and climb the social ladder despite endless obstacles put in their way. The men, though, are little more than window dressing. As played by Ecker, *Café*'s Sebastián is an impossibly beautiful man with an enviable jawline whose life feels scripted by the circumstances around him. Where Gaviota is proactive, he is mostly a passive entity to whom many of the characters around him (most tellingly his girlfriend, who is intent on marrying him for his money, and his mother, who hopes he'll take over the family business) could pin their hopes and dreams knowing he'd not protest enough. Similarly, *Betty*'s Armando—also with a conniving girlfriend on hand—is nothing more than a prop for the self-actualization of the show's female lead. Framed by some of the most conservative visions of heterosexual romance you could fathom, these stories gave some semblance of agency to their female protagonists while being mostly uninterested in the interiority of their leading men.

Even as the telenovela gets unfairly maligned as a "woman's genre," its stories make the shows perfect vehicles through which to look at the lessons these hit dramas were teaching young boys like me. Here's why *Hombres* felt so revelatory: The groundbreaking series riffed on telenovelas while borrowing freely from prime-time American dramas. Its ensemble depicted a cross section of the new kind of man who roamed the streets of Bogotá. Our lead, a redhead named Julián Quintana (Nicolás Montero) is, as it turns out, the blandest of the bunch, an everyman designed to anchor the more outlandish characters around him. There is Santiago Arango (Luis Mesa), a rampant misogynist who abuses his wife and proudly tells his friends that a fist is the best way to keep a woman in check. Then there is, as if to balance such unsavory behavior, Ricardo Contreras (Gustavo Angarita), an older man whose decades-long marriage is the kind his colleagues aspire to have, especially Tomás Holguín (Ernesto Benjumea), a mustachioed young man whose romantic aspirations are constantly sabotaged by his own desperation. Rounding out this sprawling cast of characters are Daniel Rivera (Luis Fernando Hoyos), a self-avowed womanizer with a distaste for emotional intimacy, and Simón McAllister (Orlando Pardo), the most junior of the associates, whose wife's death leaves him as a single dad of two young kids.

Compared to telenovelas with historically flattened male characters, *Hombres* was grounded in a multifaceted reality. The series tackled contemporary plots (death, divorce, AIDS, and changing sexual mores, among others), and made a point of thinking beyond romance as its central narrative engine. At times it felt more like a character study than a Colombian melodrama, as it posited inquiries into modern manhood that felt incredibly timely. And there was a familiarity at play here. My private, elite school was populated by many boys who would (and did) grow up to be the kind of men *Hombres* depicted and spoke to. These were the boys whose approval I craved and yet who amused themselves by riling me up and then mocking my emotional outbursts. "Ay, se puso salsita!" one would needle me, calling me out for losing my temper and not taking their jokes in good stride. I often hated how much I hoped to be liked by them (and, actually, how much I was attracted to some of them), but that just meant any attention I got from my schoolmates was always tinged with ill-placed jealousy and self-hatred. What was most annoying—if not outright embarrassing, for them more so than me—was the way such taunts always felt like they reinforced their own bonds. I could get along with one or two of them at a time (especially when we were assigned group lab projects or classroom presentations to work on), but there was something about their pack mentality that brought out the worst in them. They boosted each other up whenever they punched me down (figuratively, thankfully). In this, *Hombres* was just as enlightening. After all, the series couldn't escape the oppressive nature of its own gendered ideals. Its title defined an essentialist proposition that could only ever fall short for those of us who knew that notions of Colombian masculinity were defined in our absence.

One of the most successful self-help books of the 1990s opens with a line so deceptively simple it would go on to captivate the entire world: "Imagine that men are from Mars and women are from Venus." John Gray's pop-psychology take on relationship advice proposed an all too neat approach to, as its subtitle suggested, "Improving Communication and Getting What You Want in Your Relationships." Or, as its more reader-friendly later editions would put it, "Understanding the Opposite Sex." Its many chapters trafficked in catchy sound bites that depended on simple analogies like "Men Are Like Rubber Bands" and "Women Are Like Waves," or on vivid imagery like "Men Go to Their Caves and Women Talk," eventually landing on self-help guidance like "Scoring Points with the Opposite Sex" and "Keeping the Magic of Love Alive." Even if, to this day, you haven't read Gray's best-selling tome, you surely haven't escaped the ubiquity of its open-ing fable.

Going full Plato on his readers, Gray imagines a helpful story of why men and women have such a difficult time communicating with one another. Born on different planets, both "sexes" eventually found one another: Martians, making great use of their telescopes, "discov-ered the Venusians" and, after falling in love from afar, invented space travel and flew to Venus, where they were greeted with open arms ("They had intuitively known that this day would come," Gray writes, about those Venus dwellers). Upon this meeting, the differences be-tween these two groups were obvious and unavoidable. Martians and Venusians reveled in their disparities, though, and learned to live with them in mind. It was only when they flew to Earth (it's unclear why) that they "forgot that they were from different planets and were sup-posed to be different." Not even Gray's mini space opera, it seems, can escape the convenient trappings of a good telenovela-esque "selective amnesia" plot. Losing the memory of their idyllic days back in Venus living in harmony is what has led to the current conflict between men and women. Gray is here to help us all remember our differences.

Revisiting Gray's guide three decades later is an exercise in cul-tural archeology. Since it was first published in 1992, *Men Are from Mars, Women Are from Venus* has sold over fifteen million copies around the globe. It's been translated into more than forty languages. It spawned a talk show, a board game, a French stage production, and many an offshoot paperback. "I didn't develop this based on reading other people's books. I don't even read that much," he told the *Los An-geles Times* following publication, "I do everything through my own personal experience." As that same feature on the writer explained, Gray tested his theories by "listening to testimonials, and encouraging seminar-goers to express approval and disapproval by clapping and hissing." That's how he was able to find which "generalizations" (his word, mind you) worked and which didn't; the research for the book was all focused on anecdotal evidence he'd gathered over the years at his seminars. As he put it, "My source for this and the validation of my information is that this is common sense." Therein lay the very insidiousness of his claims—and the root of the animosity he engendered within the academic community. Common sense has a way of being descriptive and prescriptive in equal measure. It's an expression that naturalizes observational behaviors and then tautologizes them, letting confirmation bias take over.

The lessons in *Men Are From Mars, Women Are From Venus* trickled down to everyday conversations where the best we could do was try to reach across a wide gender divide by learning how to "speak" each other's language. It's why the book comes with ready-made translations, courtesy of a lost "Venusian/Martian Phrase Dictionary." That's how Martians knew that when a woman said, "We never go out," she didn't mean (as they initially understood it), "You are not doing your job. What a disappointment you have turned out to be. We never do anything together anymore because you are lazy, unromantic, and just boring," but rather, "I feel like going out and doing something together. We always have such a fun time, and I love being with you. What do you think? Would you take me out to dinner? It has been a few days since we went out." As Gray explains, "when a Venusian is upset she not only uses generalities, and so forth, but also is asking for a particular kind of support. She doesn't directly ask for that support because on Venus everyone knew that dramatic language implied a particular request." If it were up to me, I'd stick with Venusian communication; who doesn't love a dramatic statement that carries within it a hidden entreaty?

I'm not here to dispute Gray's claims or quibble with his methodologies—plenty of academics and writers have done so in the decades since, even as others have tried to couch his insights in scientific terms. What I am fascinated by is his creation of such a loosely sketched allegory to anchor his point; you don't need to be a literary scholar to see the many glaring holes (narrative and logistic) that riddle his quaint story about Martians and Venusians. I know I shouldn't nitpick and that Gray's worldbuilding needn't be so scrutinized but, honestly, when you're so bold as to create such a wild origin story and put it in the very first pages of your book—and make it the title of your study, no less!—you're begging us all to poke holes in your narrative. Indeed, his move into allegorical territory leaves me with more questions than answers. Why do Martians have telescopes? What other technology did they produce while living blissfully unaware of another alien race two planets over? Why did the Venusians have an inkling they'd one day be visited by a group of men who would become besotted with them? And why would they welcome them with open arms? Why, in this scenario, are Martians still doers and oglers, while Venusians are merely objects of desire? But, perhaps more to the point, why, even amid all this celebration of difference between the "sexes" are the differences *within* them so handily ignored?

Then again, that Gray's fable and book struck a chord speaks to the way readers were famished for easily distilled gender theories—the kind, of course, we've all been fed in various ways in romantic comedies, in sweeping melodramas, and yes, in many a telenovela.

To watch *Hombres* is to see a world not unlike the one painted by Gray's book. One where men and women are cut from such different cloths it's a wonder (and an everlasting mystery) how they ever find ways of living together. If telenovelas writ large were enamored with romantic plots that upheld social mores (and yes, prim and proper heterosexual pairings), *Hombres* posited a different possibility for mainstream television. Here was a conscious exploration of modern Colombian masculinity that was nevertheless not as culturally expansive as its simple title promised. The show's pilot episode, for instance, opens not with its male ensemble, but with a scene at a restaurant where we hop from table to table and listen in on several conversations women are having about the men in their lives. A middle-aged woman bemoans the fact that her husband left her for a younger woman; her friend tells her she should be lucky he was honest. Hers has been seeing someone behind her back for years and she wishes he'd just own up to it. Another wonders aloud why it seems men nowadays want the very thing they've long villainized. Don't they hate and denigrate stay-at-home moms and housewives? Why, then, do they insist now on wanting their spouses to stay home, play house, and cater to their every whim? Others pride themselves on their newfound assertiveness: "So I told him, leave," one says. "There's the door. You think I'd be the first woman to raise a kid by herself?" Another: "What I do with men is what, historically, they've done to us; I just bed them." Later, we see a young woman crying after sharing that her boyfriend wants to stay together (but still see other people) as a nearby waitress worries the guy whose baby she's now carrying may ghost her after hearing said news. As the waitress then makes her way through the dining room, the din around her takes over; every table is full of women talking about nothing but men, offering a perfect example of how to fail the Bechdel test.

The kicker for this prologue is a brief vignette focused on a young girl set against a white backdrop. She is impeccably dressed, as if styled for a family portrait, in a cutesy dark-blue sailor dress. As she plays with a ball, a young boy comes in and smacks it right out of her hand, only to laugh loudly when he gets a glimpse at her frilly bloomers as she bends down to retrieve it. The camera closes in on her as she grimaces. "Hombres!" she spits out, "Guácala!" ("Men! Yuck!").

Years before *Sex and the City* turned girl talk brunch into a tired TV trope, *Hombres* creator Mónica Agudelo understood the cultural importance of enshrining the intimacy such a setting afforded women in the mid-nineties. What's striking about these vignettes is how they neither seek to villainize men nor outright excuse their behavior. Against an entire genre that so exalted marriage, monogamy, and the nuclear family, *Hombres* set out from the start to ground us not in

the aspirational images of church weddings and picture-perfect images of wholesome happy families (the kind that littered too many a
telenovela ending) but in the messy and modern conflicts that were,
as was the case in these conversations, the talk of the town. To open
with women's complaints and to tie them to concerns about divorce,
motherhood, and courtship remains as revelatory in the twenty-first
century as it was in 1996. These may have once been private concerns,
but by staging them in a public setting like a restaurant, these groups
of female friends created a choral effect that rippled out from every
table. Agudelo made clear this series would air out stories long kept
hidden behind closed doors.

   Likewise, the modern men at the heart of *Hombres* would come
to feel oddly familiar, contemporary avatars of a generation that was
remaking the narratives around romance they'd long been fed. Stockbrokers by trade, they were associated with a cosmopolitan environment and thus a vision of Colombia that imagined the country as
economically forward-looking and ready to shed its bad rap. They
were, in many ways, grown-up versions of my own schoolmates—
many of whom would, in fact, go to Colombia's top two schools to
study Administración de Empresas, the catchall business major preferred by the country's upper class. Our school was all but a conveyor
belt toward early twenty-first-century yuppiedom. *Hombres* offered a
glimpse into a possible future and a rare window into an alien present.
For, if these stockbrokers weren't older facsimiles of my fellow classmates, they were easily legible as their fathers, who ran multinational
corporations, were executives at oil companies, or were otherwise
part of the movers and shakers in a city that was desperately trying
to rebrand itself into a future where it needn't have to be associated
with drug cartels, car bombs, and a decades-old violent conflict that
seemed to have no end in sight. Given that my mom worked in a
creative industry, those suit-and-tie men were foreign figures to me. I
knew—or gathered, more like—that I was supposed to see in them

an aspirational image, their menswear supposedly projecting a seriousness to look up to. Our school uniforms instantiated this, in fact.

Had I followed a different path in life—had I, for instance, stayed in Bogotá and gone to either Los Andes or La Javeriana for school—I'd have likely moved in circles like those depicted in *Hombres*. Revisiting the show all these years later, I am reminded, though, of why I left. For even as the show presents a wide variety of high-powered men who struggle with issues as varied as marriage, parenthood, friendship, dating, and yes, even a crazed female stalker, Agudelo's show can't—and didn't try to—escape the subtle homophobia that undergirded all its commentary on contemporary Colombian men. One that, in this case, nevertheless came wrapped up in a rather tepid push for tolerance and acceptance.

For, alongside the Juliáns and the Santiagos of the group, *Hombres* offered audiences a token gay guy. As nineties tropes required, Marcel was a limp-wristed, fashionable "gay best friend" who ran a clothing boutique and spent many evenings gabbing about with de Francisco's Antonia. And, though we first meet him having a meltdown over his recent breakup, his romantic (and sexual) life is all but nonexistent. On-camera at least. During one episode, when Antonia cancels their plans as she opts to go out on a date with Julián, we see him joking that he'll spend the evening reading *One Thousand and One Nights*, as if his social life were only tethered to her availability. He was, in a way, the Will to Antonia's Grace before that U.S. sitcom had even been conceived.

Played by Claude Pimont, Marcel was coded as different—as foreign, even. Pimont's accented Spanish (he was born and raised in France before kicking off his acting career in Colombia), not to mention his shoulder-length hair and endless collection of fancy silk scarves, set him apart from the show's cast of characters, whose clean-cut near-identical looks stressed and encouraged homogeneity.

At the end of the day, the boys club *Hombres* depicted depended on setting itself apart from men like Marcel. For, in a series known for its battle of the sexes theme, Marcel usually found himself grouped (willingly and giddily, I must add) with the girlfriends and mothers present in the show. This was nowhere more evident than in a two-part episode cheekily titled "Detrás de un gran hombre hay una gran mujer" ("Behind every great man lies a great woman"), which is centered around Julián's best friend Mafe's thirtieth birthday party. Wanting to buoy her spirits over crossing that milestone, Marcel suggests she host a raucous costume party for herself. A gender-bending party, in fact: have all the men dress up as women and all the women as men. The ladies are thrilled! At last, a chance to wear baggy suits and play at being men for a day. The boys, though, are less than thrilled. The mere concept of taking up drag for a day appalls them even as they (mostly) begrudgingly agree to take part in such a lark. The only holdout is, unsurprisingly, Santiago, who badgers and belittles his friends for letting themselves be so emasculated as they opt to wear miniskirts, makeup, wigs, and even heels.

Much of the humor of the episode centers on the inherent hilarity of seeing grown men in feminine clothing. Tomás's choice to don a wedding gown elicits plenty of quips about being a virginal bride, Julián's smoky eye makeup and fishnet stockings earn him several lady-of-the-night jokes, and the men's high-pitched vocal affectations as they role-play are all done in jest, pointing out the hilarity of what it takes to be—to become, really—a woman. In an ironic twist, though, Marcel does not arrive all dolled up in a corset and a killer wig. Instead, he arrives in full Rambo drag, all camo gear and fake guns ablaze. "I couldn't betray my inner woman," he explains, "It was easier to betray the man in me." It's hilarious to think that such betrayal involved conjuring up this particular image of a "man." He reached into the far recesses of American pop culture iconography but there was no denying the way his military garb visually invoked a Colombian reality the show otherwise kept decidedly off-screen.

Masculinity and homosexuality were, in the show's framework, not only incompatible but diametrically opposed. As this double episode illustrated, masculinity is not something you have; it is something you do. Something you perform, really. And, more crucially, something you perform for other men. It is not enough to be a man; you must act like one—and sometimes, that was as difficult for guys like Julián and his friends as it was for those of us who have become canny observers of men to better mimic them and thus hide our desire for them.

Intertwined as they were, homosexuality and masculinity were, from a young age, parts of myself I knew were overly scrutinized. The visibility of one came at the expense of the other. Both were configured in our culture as things to look out for both because they *can* be seen and because we might *not* see them. As these episodes of *Hombres* suggest, the kind of masculinity Santiago so extols is fragile precisely because it depends on its insistent visibility—it's why he doesn't dare not wear a tuxedo to Mafe's party and why he thinks a mere wig will unravel the assured sense of manhood he wishes and demands of his friends. And, while the show does nudge us toward scoffing at Santiago's retrograde ideas, the twists in the plot all but hand him a win. Shortly after leaving the party together, the men are arrested for being intoxicated. That they're suffering this humiliation while still wearing skirts and heels is almost too much—and that's before the cops tease them about their outfits. The police at the precinct all assume they are "transvestites," and thus worthy of their scorn; they throw the boys out into the gated yard, where they're further harassed by the other jailed men who are both threatened and amused. Julián worries they'll be raped and hopes they won't have to fend any men off, a line that gives them all a chance to curse Marcel again for this ridiculous idea. And, true to form, they do end up needing to fight to prove their masculinity and strength.

When they're finally picked up by the women, they bemoan their decision to have played along to Mafe's ridiculous gender-bending party, all while their fellow inmates marvel at their fighting prowess, offering the kicker that captures the incongruity of the entire scenario: "Esas locas terminando siendo unos varones!": "Those fags turned out to be quite the men!" Though perhaps *fags* isn't the right translation. For *loca* (literally "crazy") is used as a way to call out effeminacy *and* homosexuality in a way that conflates them with mental illness, and is most often used as a derogatory insult against trans and gender-nonconforming individuals, the kind who would don wigs and dresses to hit the streets at night. Though, similar to *fag*, *loca* is a term that's continually being reappropriated, used as a way to embrace the scorned femininity it's supposed to pathologize. By throwing punches and asserting their dominance in the only way they know how, these mocked men end up proving their masculinity by behaving like their most primal selves.

Throughout the show, masculinity—whether championed by Santiago's retrograde machismo or the cops' open homophobia—was constantly being negotiated by Julián and his friends. Quite predictably, the series would eventually frame such questions about masculinity in terms of violence. For that is what a *varón* is: even in a dress, if a man can beat his assailant, he can get away from hurtful labels like *loca*. As if to nurture their fragile egos, Julián and company decide on a whim to go on an all-boys camping trip, a laughable attempt to reassert whatever authority they believe had been wrestled from them. All alone, away from the prying eyes of the women in their lives, they revert (or become) the most machista versions of themselves they can dream up. At one point they go around in a circle sharing funny jokes that all depend on the gentle misogyny they feel all too comfortable performing for each other: "What does a woman do after making love? Get in the way." "What would man do without women? He'd domesticate another animal." The laughter these jokes elicit is rooted in the kind of feminist intervention *Hombres* was gunning for. The pathetic attempts by these men at finding the humor in their plight is what should make us chuckle; we're encouraged to laugh *at*, not *with* them. For, again, the storyline ends with Mafe and the girls coming to their rescue, further painting these men as hapless fools who can't go a full weekend without their every whim taken care of.

Reviewing *Hombres* upon its release in 1996, Colombian magazine *Semana* singled out how the show presented a necessary corrective to the way telenovelas had been produced in the country's history: "Although the audience for melodrama is composed mostly of women," the review argued, "in Colombia the writing of matters of the heart has always been a matter of men." Some of the biggest homegrown hits had been developed and written by a cadre of talented men who'd created a string of powerful heroines, including *Café*'s Gaviota, whose love stories had wooed and wowed audiences for generations. With *Hombres*, Mónica Agudelo was turning such tradition on its head: "Although for many it may look like a sign of a move past melodrama, the show is, on the contrary, firmly rooted within the rules of that genre, only seen with the keen-eyed outlook of a modern woman, for whom Agudelo is undoubtedly becoming, for all her merits, her new priestess."

The series was an answer to an incongruous-sounding question: What would it mean to write a male-centered telenovela? To write a melodrama about men? What emerged was a bold offering, a series that took men's inner lives seriously and dramatized that clichéd and endlessly recurring concept of the "crisis of masculinity." Though perhaps, given its plural title, we should amend its take on such a theme. Maybe *Hombres* was a series about the crises of masculinity. Or better yet, about the crisis of masculinities. If it feels like masculinity is constantly in crisis, that is because such is its very nature. It may well be that the crisis itself *is* masculinity. Or, at the very least, the patriarchal masculinity whose fragility masks the very strength it purports to project.

If the tenets of masculinity, as *Hombres* shows time and time again, are inherently performative, depending on and constantly reinscribed for and by those around us, it's hard to not both commend the show for that push and pull and to condemn it for so tactfully tackling its male protagonists. In hindsight, its attempt at satire never went far enough—and this had everything to do with the way it careened ever closer to the generic telenovela trappings it was so intent on serving up. Was this a modern dissection of the fragile masculinity that so enthralled well-to-do Colombian men? Or was it an apology for their actions, a way to not merely explain them away but validate them? The fine line between description and prescription, between representation and aspiration, can't help but be blurred when in episode after episode, *Hombres* insisted on giving its titular straight men so much empathetic leeway. This was a show, after all, that ended its series finale with the women playfully excusing the men for their shortcomings, teaching the audience an insidious lesson: "Les perdonamos su género," the women tell the men in the final tableau the show left its viewers with: "We forgive you for your gender."

4.

Pink Armor

"CAN'T I JUST BE ANGRY?!"

"Yes. But you don't need to take it out on the floor. Be angry! Just . . . do it silently."

That only riled me up more, even if it did quiet me down. Silently, I cursed how ridiculous my show of anger had been. Huffing, I'd thrown my now ex-husband's flip-flops down with a melodramatic flair. The pettiness of the gesture, not quite directed at him though obviously done for his benefit, my anger needing an audience, is what made him snap. Rather than try my hand at a response, I merely opened the door to the vestibule outside our apartment, found again no trace of the winter boots I'd just recently realized had been stolen (yes, my anger wasn't unfounded but it was also hilariously outsized), and proceeded to make my way through our building. The idea, which sounded stupider the more I thought about it, adding to my budding anger, was to check other apartment vestibules for my boots, as if they had somehow been misplaced. I hadn't made it past our floor before I came back even more frustrated.

My anger, I know, is not often silent. It's mellowed a bit, despite my then-partner's protestations. If only he'd known me as a teen.

I made the mistake a few days after the winter boots incident of bringing up, while suppressing giggles, the many ways my teen-age tantrums had resulted in, among other things, broken chairs and upended furniture. He chastised me, thinking me too flippant, before I could tell him the story of when I got so angry with my sister that I jumped up and down on her pencil case, breaking her T9 calculator in the process, before punching her door (she'd locked herself in her room, naturally) and leaving a fist-sized hole in it that matched the one I'd already punched in my own bedroom door, the result of yet another outburst directed at my younger brother weeks before. Yes, I was a walking-and-talking cartoon character whenever I was upset (my favorite Disney character has fittingly always been the cantankerous Donald Duck). Which is why people—both then and now—struggle squaring those hotheaded moments with my everyday equanimous demeanor. You could say I'm a poster boy for the stoic, silent type. My mom would often deploy this epigram, like something out of a Psalm, when explaining my temper to anyone who'd dare not believe her: "Líbrame de las aguas mansas que de las malas me libro yo." More than a saying, the line always struck me as a kind of prayer: "Deliver me from still waters; of the rough ones I'll free myself." You can fight against rapid torrents, flailing and swimming to safety in a flush of adrenaline. It's much harder to slink your way out of a still, never-ending well not knowing what it is that lurks underneath.

I wasn't always a tantrum-throwing kid. In fact, before she was regaling friends and family alike with stories about which piece of furniture I'd recently destroyed or what door would need to be replaced following my latest flare-up, my mom had a wealth of stories about how well-behaved a toddler I was. She could leave me in my playpen for hours on end and I'd barely make a sound. This was all the more remarkable, and welcome, given that my sister, born a mere twenty months later, spent much of her early years wailing her heart out. She was eventually diagnosed with a UTI, her crying a mystery solved, but she never lived down her reputation for being my rowdy foil. Later, in school, I was regularly commended by my teachers for being a quiet, studious child. In the decades since, people have added adjectives like *unapproachable, cold*, and *indifferent* to their first impressions of me, commenting that I tend to appear as though I am always at a remove from what's happening around me. I do admit I often recede into the background whenever I can, retreating to my teenage years, when all I ever felt like was a gawking audience member at a show that didn't seem scripted for me at all.

When I moved to Vancouver for college, I recast that peaceful exterior as a zen-like approach to life, shedding the repressed, anal-retentive high schooler I had been for a sarcastic, devil-may-care twenty-something who at some point became the aloof thirtysomething I am today. Give or take a flip-flop-related incident, my anger rarely bubbles up anymore. But for years, it was something I lived with, nurtured even, and then gleefully unleashed on those around me, feeding off the high of the white-hot rage radiating out of me, obliterating everything in its path. There was always something quite empowering about my tantrums. It wasn't only the attention, which I shamefully craved, especially when we visited extended family and I found myself needled and bullied by my older cousin for my lack of soccer skills, and inadvertently belittled by my aunts, who had a way of getting under my skin with their quips about my quiet softness. What was powerful in those moments was the way I felt inviolate. Watching family members recoil—maybe not in fear; in shock or annoyance, perhaps—at my red-faced, hotheaded reactions was intoxicating.

My anger was a suit of armor. Not one I donned every day and wore out in petty squabbles. But one I called up whenever I needed to feel, well, like a man. It seems silly to explain it this way now, with close to two decades of hindsight on my side. But if I'm being honest with myself, that's what drove my tantrums. My unbridled aggression in those moments was the only way I seemed to adhere to the tenets of masculinity that were expected of me. Men's anger and its attendant aggression wasn't just rewarded. As bell hooks sums it up, "Real men get mad. And their mad-ness, no matter how violent or violating, is deemed natural—a positive expression of patriarchal masculinity. Anger is the best hiding place for anybody seeking to conceal pain or anguish of spirit." Men, the world told me, couldn't be—weren't!—emotional beings. Unless they were angry. There was power to be wielded with this anger, and wills to be bent in turn. Such messaging was everywhere around me. Even—especially—in the shows I devoured as a kid.

I never noticed just how violent the television series I grew up with were. Not violent as in gory or explicit. Just in that violence was the structuring framework for many of their premises: the ThunderCats fought off Mumm-Ra; the X-Men fended off both the U.S. government and Magneto's henchmen; Tom and Jerry seemed to always be at each other's throats, and don't even get me started on the flippant slapstick comedy that made Wile E. Coyote a walking insurance liability. It's not so simple to say TV shows geared toward men glamorized or even glorified violence (the Care Bears and Sailor Moon would like a word), but it is hard not to look at this selection and wonder whether framing serialized narratives around the need to fight foes on a weekly basis was arguably the best pedagogical approach for children's TV. At least by the time I became obsessed with *Pokémon*, as kids all over the world did, you could argue I'd found a television show that at least encouraged a more collegiate and ecological approach to such narratives.

But I'm getting ahead of myself. Because before that Japanese import became an obsession of mine (as I learned on a recent trip home, my mom still has an entire box full of my collectible *Pokémon* cards), I was equally enthralled with another anime show. This one prided itself on championing a vision of ruthless aggression that was very much tied up in a decidedly rigid vision of what hooks accurately describes as "patriarchal masculinity." hooks's description is helpful in that it keeps us from falling into the trap of thinking masculinity itself is inherently violent and aggressive—precisely what patriarchal societies would like us to believe.

Yet many of the exhortations we hear about what it means to be a man rarely come with such caveats. A line like, "Keep fighting like a man until the very end," integral as it is to a television series I adored growing up, didn't ever hide the expectation it drew whenever it was uttered. Shun, a young green-haired mythical fighter who grew up in the shadow of his irascible and protective brother, slowly learns he can't run away from such an imperative. Instead, he makes it a lifelong mantra. It's a line Shun hears in his head whenever he needs to destroy the latest foe who (as many others before) has threatened to finally beat him and his friends in what was, growing up, one of my favorite television shows.

Saint Seiya (or, how I encountered it in Colombia, *Los caballeros del Zodíaco*) was structured around fighting. This is a show about the beauty and honor inherent in beating the shit out of those who get in your (righteous, obviously) way. Then again, as I noted above, I could be describing any number of hit shows in the late twentieth and early twenty-first centuries. But this was especially the case with many coming out of Japan, the ones that flooded Colombian screens, famished as our local industry was for imported content (all dubbed, of course). The shōnen genre of anime—aimed at and starring teenage boys—was rife with narratives that exalted these very "masculine" values.

Describing shows like *Teenage Mutant Ninja Turtles*, *ThunderCats*, *G.I. Joe*, and *Transformers* as the stuff of "boys" can feel like underselling both their universal appeal and ignoring their bustling fangirl base. But in Japan, the distinctions within manga publishing, shōjo and shōnen, describe two different if increasingly overlapping genres. Shōjo (literally "young woman") is aimed at a teen female demographic, while shōnen ("young boy") courts a teen male demographic. The country's more strictly gendered genres explain why you can't talk about shōnen anime like *Saint Seiya* without also talking about its depiction (and endorsement) of certain brands of masculinities. That's because, while shōjo often focuses on romantic relationships, shōnen is characterized by martial arts, sports, and mecha storylines that dramatize camaraderie among boys. Such clear gendered delineation (which didn't restrict itself to mere themes but also to the visual grammar) soon came to characterize animated adaptations of these same projects.

This was the case with *Saint Seiya*, a manga that debuted in 1986 and was already being adapted into an animated television show later that fall. *Saint Seiya* follows a group of young boys, all of whom are mystical warriors whose mission is to defend the reincarnation of the goddess Athena. This leads them to fight many an all-powerful villain throughout the course of the show's more than three hundred episodes. Each of their armors (dubbed as *cloths*, but it's best to think of them as knightly garbs) is associated with a specific constellation that grants them supernatural abilities as well as a way to tap into their inner "Cosmo" energy. The titular fighter, for instance, is the Pegasus Saint, whose meteor fists attack—as well as his unbridled bravery— make him a worthy adversary as well as a de facto leader of the Bronze Saints who make up the core group of the show. Fighting alongside him are Shiryū (Dragon) and Hyōga (Swan), as well as Ikki (Phoenix) and his younger brother Shun (Andromeda). With its spectacular fights and sprawling mythology borrowed from Greek and Nordic lore, *Saint Seiya* is a perfect example of the shōnen genre that made its way across the world in the late twentieth century courtesy of its anime adaptations.

In Colombia alone, you could watch variations on this theme on hit shows like *Dragon Ball* and its sequel *Dragon Ball Z*, which followed the affable and all-powerful Goku as he fought his way through a string of menacing baddies, as well as *Captain Tsubasa*, which substituted the superpowered fighting for a less bloody setup, following the titular character as he and his soccer team faced off against adversaries at the collegiate level and later on pro teams. While telenovelas dominated our prime time, imported animated fare ruled the afternoons. I always knew if I finished homework early (or, more likely, if I put it off until early evening), I'd have hours of anime shows to entertain me as soon as I got back from school. I was never a big extracurricular guy (I did take part in choir, where I was the sole male soprano, naturally). I didn't live near any of the scant friends I had at school, nor did I ever succeed in making friends at my residential complex. So my afternoons were spent glued to the television. Eventually, of course, I'd become obsessed with *Pokémon* (and, unbeknownst to my friends at school, I also gravitated toward teenage girl–driven shows like *Sailor Moon*). But nothing came close to how much I enjoyed *Saint Seiya* and how much I daydreamed about donning Andromeda's armor. Yes, the pink one. The one modeled after a female constellation. The one that belonged to Shun, the softest of the young fighters whose long, lush green hair and tender features got him called out for being too pretty to fight, better suited to being a movie star than a Bronze Saint. Yet he always emerged as the strongest and most resilient of them all, always returning and finding strength in his brother's exhortation: "Keep fighting like a man until the very end."

One of the reasons I so gravitated toward Shun was because, in a show that so openly celebrated fighting and aggression, he was an outspoken pacifist. He only fought as a last resort, as a begrudging means to an end. He took no joy in it (as did his brother, at times), nor did he take pride in hurting others (as did some of his foes). For him, there was more to life than fighting. But more than that, Shun was soft where his fellow warriors prided themselves on being hard. On being manly. On being boys, really.

Here Shun stood apart. As flashbacks to his childhood show us, he was bullied by those around him, an easy target for their taunts as a meek young boy who shied away from conflict and, as everyone reminded him, didn't deserve to be training alongside these rowdy boys who relished their skirmishes and saw them as a necessary part of their upbringing. Despite Ikki's pleas to "fight like a man," this beautiful young boy grows up instead to be the kind of knight who does all he can to avoid attacking anyone around him. "I don't want to fight," he tells his master trainer when pushed to defeat a fellow trainee to win the Andromeda cloth; "I prefer to defend myself," he explains later during a one-on-one battle before being egged on by Ikki once more to stop being a crybaby and attack already. The show paints Shun's reticence toward violent aggression as a noble, admirable trait that eventually earns him plaudits from his master. Yet his mere inclusion in this roster of heroes meant the show understood and, crucially, wanted to elevate Shun's own variation on the male aggression that *Saint Seiya* so celebrated.

With his soft facial features (and, tellingly, his small-breasted pink armor), Shun was a welcome role model for a gangly, awkward, soft kid who was enthralled by those hard bodies he spied at the local gym he decided to join on a whim, or the kind he encountered all over pop culture. Heck, even the kind that populated the various other anime shows he watched dutifully. Then again, anime is in a league of its own when it comes to creating improbable bodies that are as awe-inspiring as they are terrifying. To watch *Dragon Ball* or *Dragon Ball Z*, for instance, was to witness a smorgasbord of veiny muscles and bulging biceps. Goku as an adult looks like a weight lifter on steroids who makes the likes of Disney's hunkified Hercules look scrawny in comparison. The proportions in those shows, in fact, were comically absurd; in stills, Goku can sometimes look like a blown-up sex doll, each muscle group engorged to the point where its separate parts make no physiological sense. Working on a more realistic mode, the lithe and ropy bodies displayed throughout *Saint Seiya* nevertheless were visions of a masculine body taken to extremes, all taut arms and slim builds, the better to show off the light, mostly decorative armor they wore in battle. These were teenage boys after all, not that much older than I was. But while I definitely had the lithe part down, my muscles had little to no definition. Then again, no one at my school did. Perhaps like most schools in the real world, mine had few examples of the teenage heartthrobs that presumably populated U.S. hallways and shōnen manga alike.

Beautifully sculpted male (animated) bodies weren't a rarity in my nineties TV-watching diet. Shows like *He-Man and the Masters of the Universe*, *X-Men: The Animated Series*, and even *ThunderCats* paraded blush-worthy images of toned bodies across my screen. To this day, my crushes on animated Cyclops (the square-cut, impossibly ripped leader of the X-Men who's constantly on the verge of letting his laser eyes scorch everyone around him) and on Tygra (the playful Thunder-Cat who knew his way around a whip) feel like Rorschach tests revealing what my teenage self was going through, their bodies calling out to me less to tell me what I wanted to be than what I wanted to hold.

Yet there was something different about the way these bodies were drawn and treated in anime shows like *Saint Seiya*. For starters, there was a chaste eroticism to them that was seldom present in their American counterparts. As I rewatched much of the show, I was floored by the amount of ogling it encourages, as much a by-product of the genre's focus on bodies as the medium's signature stylistic grammar. Given that these manga and anime were aimed at and focused on teenage boys, finding many of their narratives centering around the body in flux is particularly apt. But here is where the very process of Japanese animation further turned the anime body into something to be carefully, obsessively observed.

For that, though, one needs a bit of history. When American animation first arrived in postwar Japan, it did so by way of Disney films on the one hand and the Fleischer brothers' projects on the other, crucially their 1940s animated take on *Superman*, which aired there in 1955. At the time, it was the first American series to be shown on Japanese television. This tale of an alien superhero whose impressive powers set him apart from the world around him went on to inspire an entire generation of Japanese animators, who began to develop an industry that, to this day, rivals Hollywood's output. Not coincidentally, it was another project about a misunderstood superpowered being that first helped Japanese animation cross over into the United States: *Astro Boy*. The show was based on one of Osamu Tezuka's breakout characters from a short-lived manga titled *Atom Taishi*, first published in the monthly magazine *Shonen* in April 1951. This animated tale of a robot who looks like a young boy marked a shift in the very aesthetics of what came to be known as anime. Or rather, a solidification of practices that had been in place but that, with *Astro Boy*, became enshrined as characteristic of the budding medium.

The famed animator had to get creative when producing *Astro Boy*, having undersold episode budgets in order to secure the production contract that would, in turn, pay dividends for all involved— infamously known as "Tezuka's curse." This led to the animation style many of us associate with anime: a blinkered vision of movement. Many of Tezuka's shortcuts entailed using (and therefore drawing) fewer shots per second, instead creating an illusion of movement through sustained pans over still shots, sometimes with added sliding background images. Which is to say, sometimes you'd be staring at the same drawing while stuff happened around it: when characters spoke, for instance, the image of the face would be still as the mouth moved; when they jumped or kicked or thrashed about, strobe-like lines would help further suggest the direction of such attacks. Or, as in an early episode of *Saint Seiya*, you'd be staring at a still image of a naked Shun seen from behind as he showers while a repeating pattern of water washes over him and the "camera" pans from his calves up to the back of his head, letting us take in his slender body in all its glory. Tezuka's limited animation style may have started as a cost-cutting gamble, but it's since evolved into an aesthetic template that dominates the way we understand the many varied projects that fall under the "anime" rubric today. This aesthetic collapses stillness and motion and thus demands a lot from individual character designs. It's why there's a dynamism to anime characters even in static frames, why muscles are so often highlighted by shadows and strained lines. You're always meant to think of them as if they were about to jump right off the screen.

These formal gambits went hand in hand with the thematic richness of many of the shows produced in the late twentieth century. Take, for instance, a series like *Ranma ½*, which straddled the line between shōnen and shōjo; this gender-fluid martial arts comedy about a young boy cursed to turn into a girl whenever he's splashed with cold water (hot water reverses said transformation) relished exploring the thorny issues of desire such a premise toyed with. *Ranma ½* was unabashedly fascinated with the titular character's body, with many a scene depending on the audience's curiosity about what lay underneath his (or her) clothes: that Ranma ends up having both male and female suitors was but one of the many ways this (yes, teen-aimed) show encouraged many of us watching to reconceptualize the way masculinity and femininity were anchored in the way we think and look at bodies. Ranma's breasts (showcased explicitly in several episodes) become an obsession of one of his crushes at school, while several nude run-ins with the girl his father has committed him to marry (much to her chagrin) highlight the ways attraction and flirtation cross over gender lines. Here gender was a malleable concept. And as Ranma shuttles between what is expected of him when he is (or merely looks like) a boy and when he is (or merely looks like) a girl, the more such distinctions became hazier and hazier.

Rumiko Takahashi may have always intended for her manga *Ranma ½* to operate as a pure slapstick take on metamorphosis folk tales ("I came up with something that might be a simple, fun idea," she's said), but her work broke apart the rigidity of gender essentialism. Ranma's storylines, so dependent on crushes and romances, on paramours and flirtations, queered the many couples the show mined for comedy. A young man falls for redheaded girl Ranma because she flouts the ways all other girls behave, the same reasons he'd first been drawn to Ranma's current fiancée, a stubborn young woman who spends her mornings handily (and almost gleefully) fending off would-be suitors. Ranma's previous fiancée, meanwhile, who'd forsaken men after their engagement was called off and had opted to live as a boy instead, ends up falling for blue-haired boy Ranma when they reunite years later after he finds her "cute." As a concept, *Ranma ½* made clear both how central and how immaterial bodies could be when it came to romantic (and yes, sexual) desires. In those American shows I mentioned earlier (let alone in those Disney films I grew up adoring), lust was rarely part of the equation. And while *Saint Seiya* was painfully indifferent to storylines around sex and romance (that being more in line with shōjo sensibilities), the show embodied an erotics of masculinity that's hard to deny.

Seiya and his friends modeled an aspirational kind of masculinity, a vision of heroics that was designed to offer guidance to the manga's young readers. For *Weekly Shōnen Jump*, the publisher behind Masami Kurumada's original *Saint Seiya* manga, titles were conceived to uphold three distinct tenets: yūjō (friendship), doryoku (perseverance), and shōri (winning/victory): "the three words reflect," chairman Hiroyuki Gotō has explained, "a positive, optimistic outlook. At *Shōnen Jump* we don't believe in the aesthetics of defeat." In the anime, Kurumada's serialized manga became a string of episodic cliffhangers that repeatedly asked viewers to wonder whether this time, unlike those ones before, would be the time when Seiya, or Hyōga, or Shun, would finally succumb. Did that poisoned rose finally kill Seiya? Did that cosmic punch finally knock out Shiryu? Will Hyōga truly freeze to death? Will a chained Shun survive the thrashing waves? And even when the answers felt obvious, there was a thrilling beauty (and a beautiful thrill) in watching our heroes dusting themselves off and eventually prevailing. Every episode, every fight, every foe became a chance

for characters and show alike to prove themselves worthy, to prove that
they, like Gotō, do not believe in the aesthetics of defeat. For *Saint
Seiya*, show and manga alike, celebrates victories above all else. "Keep
fighting like a man until the very end," as Shun's adopted mantra goes.

I grew up hearing variations of Ikki's exhortations.

"No sea marica," was easily the foulest of them all. Amassing any
and all attendant masculine anxieties, such an order (often yelled with
contempt and disgust) encouraged us boys to not be "fags," and to be
men instead. To forgo the softness of the sissy and embrace the hardness of straight men. Of *real* men. Of patriarchal men. The variation
that always tickled me was "No sea *tan* marica." The added qualitative
marker ("Don't be *such* a fag," or "*so much* of a fag") always felt unintentionally revelatory: we already had some faggotry within us; we
just all had to keep it in check. Even when I was told not to tap into
my inner fag, I was called to become a very specific kind of man: "Un
hombre tiene que ser berraco."

Berraco is a hard word to translate. First off, for Castilian Spanish speakers, the spelling should likely be *verraco*, which is a word
that describes both a boar and a series of artistic stone-carved animal
sculptures found all over Spain. With those associations in mind, it's
understandable how the word became a malleable catchall in Colombian slang to denote strength and virility. To call someone a *berraco*
is to compliment them on their savviness, a way of celebrating their
awe-inspiring accomplishments. A berraco is someone who endures
and excels. Namely, that person is a badass. Such toughness, though,
extends to its other meanings and uses. Deployed as a modifier, it
stresses your exhaustion, suggesting a sense of being overwhelmed.
Similarly, idiomatic phrases associated with it—"¡Ni por el berraco!":
"Absolutely not!" and ". . . más que un berraco": "more than a lot"—
tie it to endless, Herculean efforts. The common expression "¡Qué ber-
raquera!" isolates all of these various definitions and comes to mean
something like "That sounds amazing!" or "How awesome is that?"

But its most curious linguistic thread has to do with anger. To be *berraco* is to be irate; to *emberracarse* is to drive oneself mad, the reflexive nature of the verb gesturing already to how the fiery anger comes and is incited from within. I never knew *berraco* came from a word for a Spanish boar that's been immortalized in brutalist sculptures, but given how friends and family used it around me, it's easy to see why an animal's irascible nature and a sculpture's unmoving stance would have led to such multivalent connotations.

The semantic constellation *berraco* weaves around itself in Colombian slang is clearly at work in the imperative I've quoted above: to be a man is to be a berraco. Taking stock of the way Colombian boys are socialized into an insidious vision of patriarchal masculinity, scholar Javier Omar Ruíz Arroyave, author of *Masculinidades posibles, otras formas de ser hombres* (Possible Masculinities, Other Ways of Being Men), singled out that expression as one of several sayings that capture the kind of machismo I grew up with. Most are familiar to those outside of Colombia. "Men don't cry," "Men don't belong in the kitchen," and "Men can't help themselves" (when it comes to sex, naturally) all feel emblematic of a Western strand of patriarchal masculinity that seemingly knows no borders. But the berraco one, as Ruíz Arroyave notes, speaks to a very specific kind of Colombian rhetoric; this demand to be a berraco is a call to hardness, to toughness, to a version of masculinity that leaves no room for weakness, be it emotional or physical. In Colombia's hegemonic gender system, as he puts it, "a series of practices are aimed at cornering, for example, the human thresholds of pain, resistance, fatigue, hunger." (My translation.)

There's no way to grapple with this imperative without considering Colombia's sociopolitical context—especially in the twenty-first century, when Ruíz Arroyave first took stock of these issues. For a country that had been embroiled in a violent conflict since the late 1940s, the desire to mold young men into being hardened (if not outright inured) to violence wasn't an abstract ask. It was a tangible demand of the many teenagers who, given the country's mandatory military service, were tasked with fighting a war that had no end in sight. To be a berraco is to be proud of how much your body can endure. For itself, yes. But also for something larger than yourself.

This was the messaging *Saint Seiya* sent my way as well. Or a variation of it. In various flashbacks throughout the show, we get glimpses of the grueling training that led each of the young warriors to look like ripped action heroes. Never, though, do these montages feel inspiring. They are primarily framed as tortures endured to prove their strength, their worth, their power. Images of Seiya bleeding while trying to break a rock with his bare hands, of Shiryu kicking and punching a waterfall to no avail, and of Shun fending off strong riptides by the sea while being chained to earn his namesake Andromeda cloth are examples of the ways these boys' bodies were pushed to their limits. The battles themselves are even bloodier and crueler, constantly calling them to fight within an inch of their lives. No match is ever complete without someone fainting from exhaustion or nearly freezing to death or collapsing on the spot after a blood-splattering punch or kick. But therein lies their strength, their heroism, really. Their heroic feats, which they wear on their body proudly with every new scar and wound, are intimately tied to their masculinity.

Ranma and Shun stood out to a young anger-filled (and -fueled) kid precisely because their vision of masculine strength made room for femininity—depended on it, almost. Which was rare and welcome. Their shows (and the shōnen genre, in general) may well have subscribed to quite rigid gender ideals, but these two characters came to represent a subversive androgyny. Unsurprisingly, there's a particular label for these types of boys. *Bishōnen* refers to a young man of extraordinary beauty (often extremely capable) who can, at times, be mistaken for a woman in appearance. Emerging from the shōjo genre, and presenting a decidedly different template of masculinity than that presented in shōnen anime and manga, bishōnen can be understood as the archetypes that have come to dominate J- and K-pop, where soft features and ripped muscles aren't so much contradictory as complementary expectations.

In the same string of episodes where we learn of Shun's cruel training, we watch him fighting—as an episode title informs us—"Warrior of Beauty! Aphrodite." Like Shun, whose constellation associated him with a mythical damsel in distress, the knight who oversees the Pisces house is tied to arguably the most famous and beautiful woman in Roman mythology. And, like Shun, the character design for them stressed Pisces/Aphrodite's feminine features. With pink-hued lips, a beauty mark, big blue eyes, matching long baby-blue locks, and a penchant for using roses as his preferred choice of weapon, there's no ignoring the gender coding happening on-screen. Moreover, Aphrodite happily plays off how he is perceived: he knows he'll be underestimated. It's why Seiya runs headfirst into a bed of roses before realizing they aren't mere decoration but a poisoned trap to keep him and Shun from advancing to the final boss of this Zodiac-themed storyline. Beauty, Aphrodite posits, can be as deadly as brute force. There can be strength in poise too.

At a time when masculinity felt like an ill-fitting outfit that made me feel wholly inadequate when I dared put it on, I looked to characters like *Saint Seiya*'s Shun. All those things I was called to associate with masculinity—strength, yes, but also power, bravado, and even anger—were here being rearranged, patterns cut and sewn in different ways. Distinctions between femininity and masculinity, between emotional excess and laconic restraint, made no sense when staring at beautiful Shun unleashing his chains on his opponents, driven by the conviction that fighting was but a final recourse to be used solely to protect those you care for. Shun felt like a fissure, a way not out but around the masculine ideals that were peddled around me. The ones that demanded I be a berraco, that I fight like a man. That I not be—which is what I always heard and knew to be true—a maricón.

5.

Of Capes and Men

WHEN MY PARENTS SEPARATED, MY FATHER KEPT ALL OF our family albums, tomes filled with a bounty of photographs from my childhood. When he died shortly thereafter, the albums stayed with his side of the family, who refused (or didn't see fit, depending on whom you ask) to return them to my mother. To us. For more than a decade those snippets of my earliest childhood memories were, in a word, lost. And, without a camera of our own, the sense that one's own life is to be captured in snapshots that you revisit so as to reacquaint yourself with those recollections was never part of my upbringing.

When the albums finally made their way back to our home, a belated if still frosty attempt by my father's family to rekindle a non-existent relationship once my sister and I were in our late teens, I stared in awe at the young boy whose childhood had been so carefully documented. Every new photograph—there were hundreds, collected in seven leather-bound albums—was a window into who I'd once been, like meeting an old friend you'd neglected for years but who found a way to make you feel like no time had passed. Staring at this exhaustive chronicle of my life from chubby newborn to unwittingly sassy six-year-old, in pools and on llamas, at school and at amusement parks, celebrating Halloweens and Christmases, felt like piecing together parts of me I'd suppressed. Here I was limp-wristed in a red Speedo. There I was smirking while lounging on a leather couch. Here I was rocking a Mickey Mouse costume. There I was giddily going to town on an ice cream cone.

The one photograph I return to time and time again, though, is harder to reframe as a gay origin story. I must be three, maybe four years old. I'm standing on a windowsill; whoever took the picture was on a balcony or a terrace just outside. I have a big grin on my face. My arms are up, mimicking an unmistakable pose. It helps, though, that I'm wearing a felted Superman costume, more likely a pair of pajamas than an actual Halloween ensemble. It's clear I'm living my fantasy. Looking into that young boy's wide-eyed grin, I can almost grasp his unbridled sense of freedom. With a cape, I felt inviolate. Fearless, even. Like I could fly. Like I could imagine a future that wouldn't go on to include a bitter divorce battle, a fatherless upbringing, a traumatic coming out, and, in a full-circle moment, yet another bittersweet divorce.

There's a special kind of magic in a cape.

Once a symbol of opulence favored by royals—a fitting correlation given how anti-utilitarian the cape has since become—it is now most famously associated with superpowered beings. There is no Superman without his S-embroidered cape, nor Batman without his signature cowl/cape combo. In comic books (Edna Mode be damned) capes are a must. They're a symbol of strength. As a fashion choice they are a visual reminder that those who sport them are decidedly different beings. On the page, capes clearly serve a purpose. To suggest flight, their creases and folds capture a sense of dynamism. They help broaden a character's visual footprint. Untethered to the physics of real-life capes, they take over full spreads, operating like extensions of the heroes in question, at times expanding themselves to increase a sense of menace, at others reducing themselves to becoming visual metonymies of these crime fighters. But capes, let's face it, are also a badass reminder that these characters were not to be fucked with. Emma Frost's cool fur-trimmed adornment was as much a fashion statement as it was a red-hot warning sign, while the cloak of levitation lent Dr. Strange an unlikely cheeky sidekick of a garment that also rounded out a killer ensemble.

When it comes to accessorizing villains, from Bela Lugosi in *Dracula* and the Evil Queen in *Snow White and the Seven Dwarfs* to Darth Vader in *Star Wars* and Ian McKellen's Magneto in the *X-Men* films, a cape has a way of connoting power, a remnant of circus strongman costumes. In the arms (or shoulders, I guess) of a certain villain, a cape could even have an added flair. Disney is known for this. One need only think of *Aladdin*'s Jafar or *Pocahontas*'s Governor Ratcliffe, two characters with swishy capes that coded them as both strong and imposing as well as flouncy and effeminate.

As with the wrestling singlet, there's a porousness to the gendered concept of a cape—especially when divorced from those superpowered beings. The drama of a cape can easily make your character a swoon-worthy hunk (see Yul Brynner in *The Ten Commandments*) or a foppish dunce (Colin Firth in *Shakespeare in Love*), a strong-willed diva (Eve Harrington in *All About Eve*) or an androgynous punk rocker (the titular hero of *Hedwig and the Angry Inch*). Add to that the way capes were central to my social studies classes, where it felt like every other week we were called to sketch indigenous warriors and chiefs whose robes lent them the air of authority along with their jeweled ensembles, and what you have is quite a versatile a garment, one equally at home in military trenches as at the opera.

Perhaps given its simplicity (when not beaded or lined) the cape is also the easiest way for kids to play make-believe. You may not be able to fly or wield a mythical hammer, but a sheet (or a towel or anything else you had at your disposal) could be wrapped around your neck and help you imagine what it would be like to scour the skies for villainous foes. When retelling *Sleeping Beauty* to my uncle, I'd used a travel blanket to better mimic Maleficent's fabulous entrance and capture the sheer drama of her being, which was, if you really distill it, a ravishing cape with a pair of horns. A cape can be transformative, a symbol that can conjure up superpowered strength or the deliciously uppity antics of a diva.

Photos from my teenage years are rare. Nonexistent, even. It was my father who chronicled our every outing; my mom, preoccupied as she was about keeping us fed and well taken care of, found little time to document our childhoods (something my younger brother, the video artist of the family, I think secretly begrudges, especially when he sees how many inane pictures of my sister and I are in those leather-bound albums). Of the handful of photos from my teenage years, the most striking are from our school's production of *The Crucible*, stills shot for the yearbook, no doubt. Like that Superman pic, I'm here yet again sporting a cape. My tenth-grade English teacher, a round-bellied, rosy-cheeked Englishman who was still adjusting to life in Colombia, single-handedly decided our school was done with musicals. We would put on a play instead. No matter that much of the audience (read: our parents, many of whom, like my mom, had only passing knowledge of key English phrases) would be less likely to follow an English-language production when not framed within a well-known story with flashy musical numbers. In years past, productions had included *Alice in Wonderland*, *Oliver!*, *The Wizard of Oz*, and, perhaps most bafflingly, *Bugsy Malone*. No matter, a straight play it would be. One as far afield from those candy-colored musical extravaganzas as one could find. For we were tasked with bringing to our makeshift stage (we had no auditorium; the cafeteria doubled as our theater) a classic American text about fragile male egos and mass sexual hysteria.

Even then, *The Crucible*, which is set during the Salem witch trials of the 1690s and was inspired and written in response to the

Communist witch hunts of the 1950s, felt like an odd choice for a Colombian school production in the early 2000s. But, as with much of our curriculum, the choice was premised on a cosmopolitan sensibility. Alas, that just meant we spent much of our IB English classes reading British and American classics written by men, suffered through endless modules on twentieth-century European conflicts in our history lessons, and all but ignored Latin American history (in general) and Colombian culture (in particular) in every single class, Spanish lit excepted. We were to become citizens of the world, though I now wonder why that always came at the expense of being actual citizens in and of our country.

Not that my seventeen-year-old self was concerned with such matters. I craved the worldliness the school and its International Baccalaureate program provided; by reading the likes of Miller and Tennessee Williams and Henrik Ibsen and Friedrich Dürrenmatt (we read a lot of drama), I could project myself outward, away from a school, a city, a country that felt more alien to me the older I got. With *The Crucible*, the drama nerds among us felt a thrill about being a part of (finally!) an adult-sounding production. Alice and Dorothy and Oliver were child's play. Even *Bugsy Malone*, the most obscure of them all, was a musical about gangsters who pie each other in the face. Here, though, was a play about adultery! And witchcraft! And trials! About the sacrifices a man makes to keep his dignity. About how fears surrounding female sexual agency could be weaponized and ultimately used to destroy a town, a marriage, a man.

Even before I auditioned, I knew which part my teacher had in mind for me: Deputy Governor Thomas Danforth. He's the villain of the piece. That's how I saw him, at least. He's male authority incarnate, rigid and stubborn to a fault. By the time it's clear the young girls he believes to be witches have been leveraging their accusations to settle petty personal matters, he refuses to admit he's been duped, instead moving forward with a string of executions of clearly innocent people,

John Proctor—the play's protagonist—among them. It's hard not to wonder what it was about my demeanor that convinced my teacher I would be a good fit for Danforth, whose supercilious arrogance so dominates the latter half of the play. He was all menace; in my hands, he was a scowl made flesh who towered over everyone around him. Literally. Onstage, my chair and desk were set on a raised platform, the better to project the way I lorded over the lives of everyone who came in front of me.

I did take to him quite effortlessly. In those production pictures I look uncharacteristically self-possessed, the stage—or the character, more like—bringing out something I was more comfortable keeping tucked away. I was never one to seek the spotlight. But becoming someone else was not just comforting, it was painfully familiar. Acting is all I did every day. I'd slowly deadened who I knew myself to be, learning to lower my voice here, hold my wrist steady there, avoid flailing while jogging here, keep my excited squeals in check there. Oh, and most importantly, playacting the part of a shy, bookish teenager who had occasional crushes on the most unassuming of the girls in our class. Such performances, which remain all too familiar to queer kids then as now, are exhausting. And angering; you're often so focused on the cosmetic trappings of your put-on heterosexuality that you forget what you're doing is actively denying yourself the freedom to be who you are. Day in and day out such calibrated gestures curdle inside you, making you irascible and, in time, perhaps, perfectly suited to play a sullen judge ready to unleash his righteous ire on all those around him.

There was something quite liberating about spewing Danforth's angry words all over the stage and then getting plaudits for my performance (and the hilariously affected British accent I'd decided was a perfect character choice) after curtain call. But, and this was me at my shallowest, what I loved most about playing Danforth was that he wore a cape. I imagine this was a nod toward judges' robes, but perhaps it was the kind of costume flourish a high school would devise when trying to capture seventeenth-century Puritans on the stage. I didn't care. All I cared about was that my costume had this long, flowing cape that made me feel invincible. In rehearsals, I relished the chance to swish it around. I loved how it billowed behind me as I crossed stage right and how it punctuated a particularly heated line reading ("Hang them high over the town! Who weeps for these, weeps for corruption!"). In my head, it lent me the strength of Batman's cowl and the suave trappings of *Sailor Moon*'s aptly named Tuxedo Mask. In sum, the cape made me feel fabulous, like I could take up more space (onstage and off) than I had ever dreamed of.

I wasn't the only one who saw the power of the cape. One of my fellow cast members, a classmate who had always nursed a somewhat unhealthy competitiveness with me (one-sided, it must be noted), soon tried to wrangle one for himself, as he was playing Reverend Samuel Parris, a groveling stalwart figure in Salem. Silently I fumed; of course he couldn't let me have this one thing. But outwardly I at least got to enjoy that while mine was floor-length, he had to settle for a hip-length one. This is what happens when you only give the costume department two days' notice for such a petty request.

I enjoyed the histrionics the cape afforded me while onstage. I may have been trying to evoke the imperiousness of Darth Vader or the menacing presence of Lugosi's Dracula, but I was surely also channeling campier figures. By the time I was in my teens, I was more likely to associate capes with the fabulousness of Freddie Mercury in his oversized, fur-trimmed "Bohemian Rhapsody" ensemble and, perhaps more to the point, with the most fashionable cape-wearing icon Puerto Rico has ever produced. Because let's face it, you can't really talk about capes without talking about Walter Mercado.

No other public figure has understood the aesthetic and performative potential of the cape as well as Walter Mercado. If you only have the most rudimentary knowledge of the Puerto Rican astrologer,

you likely know about his fanciful outfits, about the dazzling Liber-
ace-esque opulence he projected while delivering daily horoscopes to
households not just across Latin America but all over the world. To
describe any one of his outfits on the page risks underselling them.
They demand to be gawked at. Not written about. But, to give you an
idea of what we're dealing with if you've never witnessed the full Walter Mercado experience, such descriptions are necessary. One must
start with his face. With his perfectly plucked arched eyebrows and
blowout blond hair, Walter often looked like a well-groomed sales attendant stylistically stuck in the 1970s. His hands, always covered
with oversized jewels and rings, served as his de facto props. He'd
dramatically use them to frame his face when he wasn't deploying
them in some vogueing-meets-QVC gestures. Around his neck you
were as likely to find a satiny, shiny tie as you were a heavily bejeweled
brooch. Excess was always the word with Walter. His capes, some of
which could weigh as much as fifteen pounds, would have swallowed
anyone else whole. But even when they were floor-length or carried
shoulder pads that aggrandized his five-foot-nine frame or, as was the
case on several occasions, they came equipped with Ziegfeld Follies–
esque neck adornments that made him look like a *Looney Tunes* title
card, Walter was always poised. In control. He made the outfit, never
the other way around. Whether the capes had thousands of encrusted
Swarovski jewels or enough feathers to have deplumed an entire me-
nagerie or painstakingly applied golden embellishments that recalled
the grandeur of Versailles, Walter was front and center, as if his outfits
were extensions of himself. If Walter's capes are considered legendary, it is because they felt like a distillation of the enthralling, kitschy
style he carefully curated, one that didn't only reflect his persona but
helped constitute it.

"I am the picture and the cape is my frame." That's how Walter
succinctly put it in *Mucho Mucho Amor: The Legend of Walter Mercado*
(2020). The posthumously released Netflix documentary benefited

from a wealth of candid interviews with the famed astrologer in his home in San Juan, a rare level of access given Walter had (mostly) been gone from the public eye since a fraught legal battle with his former representation in 2006. And even though some of his witticisms have the well-worn feel of a rehearsed bon mot, their truthfulness remains no less convincing. For to think of himself as a picture that requires—nay, demands—a frame is to hear Walter articulate his own sense of artistry. Walter understood the magic of a great cape. Lending him the air of a sorcerer supreme headed to an opera premiere, his outfits helped bracket him from the everyday lives his viewers led. No one looked like Walter. On- or off-screen. That despite this high-drama style he found a way to be relatable, speaking directly to the camera as if he were talking to you specifically, was arguably the reason his *Primer Impacto* segments on Univision were big hits.

To this day, I am very much an astrology agnostic. Other than somewhat enjoying the idea that being a Libra means I am prone toward balance (gray was my favorite color as a teen, but perhaps that had more to do with a flawed conflation of color with flamboyant homosexuality than wanting to embrace the midpoint between black and white), I have never put much stock in constellations and arbitrary calendrical divisions. That didn't stop me from reading my horoscope in the newspaper every morning. Or consulting the end-of-the-year predictions printed by glossy mags in December. It was just something you did. For, despite Colombia being quite a religious country (I did my first communion and my confirmation through school), there's always been a welcome commingling of Catholic pageantry with the more outré spirituality Walter preached.

Indeed, to watch Walter was to witness a haphazardly put together mélange of teachings and doctrines. He talked of "God" but never in a specific way. He borrowed heavily from Eastern religions and Afro-Caribbean Santería. His believers—those followers who watched him religiously, attended his in-person events, bought his books, and called his 1-800 number to get personalized readings—took kindly to his penchant for generalized predictions ("Pon tu la luz en este momento de tu vida") and placid platitudes ("El amor es el alfa y el omega"). The aura around Walter was hard to parse then and harder still to explain now. There was his charisma, yes. But it is still baffling—in all the right ways—why such machista societies so embraced him.

Not that him being universally beloved meant he was beyond mockery. Two images—one of Walter as a well-respected astrologer fawned over by television hosts and the other as fodder for skeezy sketches on those same television networks—were so intertwined in Latin American television in the late 1990s and early 2000s I can't untangle them in my mind. One was always tinged by the other. It may not surprise you to hear that in those supposedly hilarious skits, Walter was reduced (by the likes of Eugenio Derbez, now an established star in the United States and at that time a bankable comedian with a late-night sketch show in Mexico) to a flouncing, lisping, limp-wristed drama queen. In *Mucho Mucho Amor*, Derbez himself looks back fondly at his impersonation. He notes that it remains one of his most treasured characters, the one fans will cite when going up to him. By his estimation, this was because his fans could see the way his spoof (named Julio Esteban) was a loving tribute to Walter. The documentary only gently pushes back, having some talking heads acknowledge how little Walter himself cared for these types of impersonations. But to revisit those sketches—or, as I did, to have grown up with them—is to see such subtle (if unintended) homophobia at work that it's hard to take Derbez at his word and not see a blatant attempt, if not at rewriting history, then at gently massaging it to soften its blow.

Everything that made Walter fabulous is what made Julio Esteban ridiculous. The pompadour wig; the bedazzled knife with his initials that he wore as a brooch; the over-the-top outfits (including neck pieces shaped as butterfly wings or covered in red petals); the affected

lilting when addressing viewers at home—these all made Derbez's Julio Esteban a punchline. And Derbez milked every effeminate stereotype to wring laughs out of his crew (whose raucous responses scored
his every sketch), giving Julio Esteban a pet peacock, exaggerating
his hand gestures to show off his bulky rings, and even bastardizing
Walter's signature catchphrase into a crude bit of toilet humor: "When
you're sad and things don't go your way," he lisps at the camera all
while mimicking Walter's gestural sign-off, "remember: take your
laxative and you'll see. You'll get rid of everything, everything you
don't need." This kind of humor was ever-present in Latin American
popular culture. Telenovelas like *Hombres* (where Marcel was a more
sympathetic version of this caricature) and *Yo soy Betty, la fea* (which
featured a high-pitched drama queen of a fashion designer) were never
above making effeminate men comedic punching bags, brought out
whenever a cheap laugh was within reach. The message was always
clear: there was a right way to be a man, and there was a laughable
way to be one. The latter was trotted out in order to consolidate the
former. When I found myself ashamed of watching Walter, the lesson seemed clear: masculinity needed to always be defined by what
it was not. Men didn't wear opulent rings. Men didn't have dulcet,
lilting voices. Men weren't vain enough to sculpt their faces and their
eyebrows. Men didn't wave their hands so much. And, of course, men
didn't wear embroidered opera capes.

Like many gay men before me, these were lessons that were so
obvious they became road maps. A way to avoid being called out for
what I lacked. Or, rather, for that performed masculinity I wanted
so desperately to run away from yet fascinated me to no end. In the
complicated gender math presented to me on a daily basis, effeminacy and masculinity were inversely proportional, and effeminacy
and homosexuality were equals, if not one and the same. Walter was
an obvious target for mockery and harassment (and, in my case, for
knee-jerk shame) because he was so unapologetically himself. But also

because he seemed to both exceed and defy the gender categories that undergirded the jokes at his expense.

When I think back to my younger self bashfully switching channels whenever Walter came on, all I see is a teenager terrified that the glimmer of recognition he saw reflected from Walter's gaze would undo him. Here was someone who clearly didn't live a life of performance—or, rather, a life of performance that depended on dulling parts of yourself to fit in. Everything I tried to suppress in myself was something Walter had not only nurtured but managed to own, celebrate, and yes, monetize. But rather than take that as the lesson to be learned, I allowed the mockery and eye rolls he elicited to guide me away from him instead. He could've been a beacon; I treated him instead like a spotlight. Better to look away from it with mock nonchalance (and very real embarrassment) than to let myself be warmed by his light.

Mucho Mucho Amor, released mere months after his death, was a chance to reacquaint myself with Walter. Not as a closeted teen running away from all things flamboyant but as an out thirtysomething-year-old who may not rock capes but has slowly been chipping away at the lessons on rugged and rigid masculinity Walter flouted with gleeful pride. The documentary, clearly produced by fans who want to reclaim him for a new generation and regift him to generations who missed him dearly, is one of the most high-profile interventions in the grand reassessment of Walter.

In addition to myself, it seems, there are now several academics and cultural thinkers who have been digging into the Walter Mercado phenomenon. Whether he's being read as a contradictory figure given his conservative and assimilationist politics or a radical queer figure whose performance of camp is ripe for examination, social studies on Walter run the gamut. To unpack what Walter meant, means, or can mean—to Latin Americans, to queer academics, to U.S. Latinos, to the LGBTQ community, to Puerto Ricans, to astrology fans, to media scholars, you name it—is to come face-to-face with an almost impossible task. Semantically, Walter is too much. His affectations and his wardrobe, like his cadence and his teachings, are so over-determined yet lacking any internal coherence—they come together only at the moment of performance—that to dissect him is to already admit defeat.

In her book *The Archive and the Repertoire: Performing Cultural Memory in the Americas*, performance studies scholar Diana Taylor spends an entire chapter on Walter. Artfully describing his stylistic flourishes ("He loves his words, he caresses them, rolling them around in his mouth") and his appeal ("He is everywhere and nowhere, visible yet uncategorizable. He is a crossover artist who exuberantly performs the space of liminality and alternativity"), Taylor wrestles with how to write about a public figure who's so slippery, one who seems anchored solely by his own gravitational pull. "As a performer," she elaborates, "Walter specializes in the art of reversal, exaggeration, conflation, contradiction, Camp, *lo cursi*, rasquache and relajo." To connect him to that cloying sentimentality that *cursi* and Chicano *rasquachismo* call up is a helpful way to begin untangling the many contradictions he embodied. It's exactly what makes Walter such a fascinating figure. He has an earnest regality, an almost religious aura about him, yet his glittering style slots him into a queer sensibility that destabilizes any set or known categories. Which is to say, there's always a lot happening when he pops on-screen and coos his astrology readings into the camera. Excess, after all, was always the beginning and end of his sense of style and sense of self. But Taylor goes further: "He endows the drag queen with papal authority." As a line, this is fabulous. And it does seem to build on those contradictions she sketched out before. Walter's persona, though, is perhaps too earnest to be dubbed camp, even as he's been co-opted into camp discourse by millennials whose memes and merch have vaulted him into internet icon territory. Likewise, *drag queen* is not entirely accurate. For drag queens exaggerate gender expression. Their giant wigs, their extended lashes, their over-the-top makeup, and outsized silhouettes call attention to all aspects of femininity, mocking and celebrating them in equal measure. That's not quite what Walter's capes and jewels and blowout are doing. More than accentuating his femininity, these trappings created a near-androgynous look. This explains why, in *Mucho Mucho Amor*, actor and influencer Curly Velasquez compares him to a "nonbinary and asexual" figure, the kind that, if he were doing astrology readings in this day and age, would be the biggest thing on Instagram.

To me, Walter's appearance feels like an expression of his personal ethos. In his 1997 book *Beyond the Horizon: Visions of the New Millennium*, Walter set out to offer guidance on what to expect at the turn of the century. Rooted in his mishmash of television teachings, *Beyond the Horizon* was premised on the coming transition from the Age of Pisces into the Age of Aquarius, a seismic shift that, according to the famed astrologer, would usher in a vastly different world order. Walter writes about how Nostradamus's conviction that this new age will mean a break with organized religions has usually also been read as suggesting "that the feminine aspects of God, which have been ignored, neglected, and reviled for the entirety of the Age of Pisces, will again be recognized and revered." Yet what he foresees will happen is not an inversion or a reversal but a commingling: "Now society," he adds, "will come to terms with the divinity of both masculine and feminine aspects, of Mother Earth and Father Sky, of yin and yang, and of the synthesis of energies for a more balanced worldview." These are ideas Walter returns to time and time again. God, he writes, "is neither man nor woman . . . [they are] the union of all the energy in the universe," arguing that "in the natural order of the universe, energy flows with both masculine and feminine force, in combination." What the new millennium would usher in, he believed, was a way to move beyond this duality, to understand that such thinking goes against the tenets of the universe, even if that's how we've been told our world is structured. "Now comes the time of integration," he further notes, "between the masculine and feminine once again. The unifying energy of Aquarius puts an end to the dichotomy of the past. There will be no more differences, no more differentiation, no more opposites. Now, not only do women want to be seen as equal to men, but men want to recapture that aspect of their nature. Once again comes the blending of the spiritual energies within us and the integration of both aspects of the divinity inside each of us, for the benefit of all humanity."

With more than two decades' worth of hindsight, Walter's all but oppressive optimism can read a tad quaint. But that was who he was. With a philosophy that was rooted, if nothing else, in the sheer power and potential of love, these pronouncements can be read less as predictions and more as aspirations. If the world was to change drastically once the clock hit midnight on December 31, 1999, why not dream up one that would be an improvement? Why not preach that here was an opportunity to do away with the cages of gender essentialism and embrace instead a welcome plurality?

Two decades after Walter's Y2K pronouncements, the astrologer's ideas about gender fluidity began to finally (belatedly, really) break into the mainstream. The number one searched-for celebrity on Google in 2019 when it came to red carpet looks, for instance, was none other than Billy Porter. The Emmy Award–winning *Pose* star turned heads at the Oscars in a custom Christian Siriano look that can best be described as a tuxedo dress and wowed onlookers at the Met Gala when he arrived in a glittering gold bodysuit by The Blonds while being carried by a bevy of beautiful men, but he kicked off that year's red carpetry with a statement ensemble that signaled the groundbreaking fashion that would follow.

Nominated for a Golden Globe at the 2019 ceremony for his role as ballroom emcee Pray Tell, the actor knew he had to make a statement. As he's explained since, Porter rarely topped designers' lists of who they'd lend their wares to at red carpet events. Not that he was an unknown commodity at that point; he'd already won a Tony and a Grammy for his role as Lola in the Broadway adaptation of *Kinky Boots*, a workplace musical set in a flailing shoe factory where his character extols the emancipatory power of a pair of well-constructed knee-high boots. And so for his most high-profile red carpet event yet, he turned to Randi Rahm. She designed him a custom hand-beaded and embroidered jacket, which she paired with a painstakingly put-together pink-lined cape that turned the *Pose* star into an instant fashion icon. Draped over his light-gray suit (worn with a sheer, equally ornamented shirt), the flower-embroidered champagne cape made Porter look impossibly regal. Photos of Porter riding a golf cart on his way to the event, his cape carefully draped behind him, stressed the majestic imagery his ensemble called forth, like he was some fabulous dignitary deigning to be shuttled to the Beverly Hills Hotel. And yet it's those images of Porter playfully and fiercely using his cape as a photo-op prop that truly made this one of the most talked about outfits of the night—no easy feat when the likes of Timothée Chalamet (in a Louis Vuitton harness), Regina King (in a pink-hued metallic Alberta Ferretti dress), and even Lady Gaga (in a cloudlike Cinderella Valentino gown, no less) walked alongside him.

The flash of hot pink from the lining begs to be called out as over-the-top (as *The Hollywood Reporter* did), making the entire look feel like it's too much. But in that giddy sense of excess Porter found his sweet spot. Liberace may have once used his bejeweled capes as performative armor on those Vegas stages and Walter may have used his equally outlandish ones as frames for his own over-the-top on-air persona, but it was this sartorial choice that allowed Porter to take up space, to assert himself in a way that announced he wouldn't be playing by anyone's rules but his own.

In one photo (by Frazer Harrison) you find him with his arms wide open, the hot-fuchsia lining framing his entire body, letting the cape serve as an extension of his own self. Porter twirled and spun with his cape, like a giddy kid finally able to show off their brand-new costume. And there was a sense of childlike wonder in Porter's twirls, as if he'd finally allowed that young queer black boy from Pittsburgh to be who he'd always wanted to be, letting flowers and a pink cape be necessary accessories to a stylish twist on that most stalwart of men's fashion. As Rahm explained, the ensemble was "a combination of muted, patterned sartorial menswear fabrics combined with the world's most luxurious couture fabrics." It was the most high-profile instance yet of Porter using red carpet appearances to, as Rahm put it, send a collective message "to the world regarding the fluidity of fashion, tolerance and acceptance"—something that would become both a mantra and a purpose for the *Pose* star.

Like Walter's capes and the type of blurring of the mere concepts of masculine and feminine such garments exalt, Porter's fashion choices have aimed at disrupting the expectations of men on red carpets. "I used to get frustrated that women could wear whatever they wanted and men had to show up in the same penguin suit," he told *InStyle* in 2021. "The reason why women wearing pants is considered OK by society's standards is because it comes from the patriarchy. The patriarchy is male, so suits are strong, and anything feminine is weak. I was sick of that discussion, and I knew my platform allowed me to challenge it." That his Oscar tuxedo dress look was an homage to ballroom icon Hector Xtravaganza, a nod both to the scene *Pose* so fabulously captured on-screen and to the many gender-bending pioneers that had come before him, allowed Porter to stand as an instantiation of the power of fashion that was forward-looking yet rooted in a long lineage of queer icons who'd been disassembling gender normativity for generations.

Not all heroes wear capes. But it's hard to ignore the power ordinary people who wish to do extraordinary things find in such a simple garment. You can spin an entire tale out of said fabric. "Gender is a story," nonbinary poet and performer Alok Vaid-Menon says, "not just a word." And so much of any one of our stories is tied up with fashion. With what we wear. Where we shop. What we dare try on and what we dare *not* put on. How we tell the story that is our gender necessarily calls us to pilfer our closets to better break out of them. If we are to embrace Vaid-Menon's dictum that there are as many ways to be a man as there are men ("This complexity is not chaos, it just is," they explain), we would do well to heed the example of the likes of Walter and Billy, one cape at a time.

6.

Walk Like a Loaded Man

In June 2017 I inadvertently began what became a long-running thread of Ricky Martin photos. I was fascinated with the Puerto Rican pop superstar's increasingly thirsty content and took it upon myself to haphazardly catalog it. The first photo I cribbed from Instagram and cross-posted to Twitter was admittedly abstract. Taken from above, it only featured Ricky's feet. Oh, and a pair of black Calvin Klein briefs, which you had to imagine had previously, perhaps even just moments before, been pulled down. So casually were they strewn around his ankles. A rainbow refracted above his toes completed the image. Caption: "Up close with this rainbow," followed by a rainbow emoji, foot emoji, and "#nofilter." For the next two years, I'd screenshot Instagram Stories where he grabbed his crotch while trying on some pants or showcased his bod in just a pair of white shorts in a mirror selfie, and I'd add the pic to the thread.

The practice became a kind of distraction. But also an unprompted examination of Ricky's persona. I eventually stopped, though on occasion I do repost some of his more delectable photos to my own Instagram Stories, a way to find kinship with others who are as likely to revel in Ricky's own revelry. One of my recent favorites is a black-and-white photo where Ricky is wearing only a pair of black briefs.

Standing slightly to the side, Ricky may be in a dressing room but it's clear the dressing part has yet to take place. He looks, there's no denying it, impossibly fit. His pectorals, accentuated by the room's overhead lighting, are lovingly defined. As are his abs. His shoulder and arm tattoos, distracting as I've long found them, here add some welcome texture to his body; such is the beauty of black-and-white photography. The shot has the air of a candid. Yet it's so perfectly framed that I have to imagine it was painstakingly staged. As was the companion pic posted alongside it. In the first he's pulling a pant leg onto (or off, maybe?) his right leg. The pair of images had been posted as promo for his appearance at the 2020 Latin Grammys ("let's do this!!!" read the caption). When you run an account that reaches more than sixteen million followers, every post is a marketing strategy, every image a PR move, no matter how candid it may appear.

What was being sold here? What was being advertised? Well, Ricky's body, for starters, as stand-in and synecdoche for his entire performance persona. But it's not as simple as saying, "Sex sells." For while these images are projecting and depending on the erotic pining of Ricky's fans, they are also asserting the star's ownership of his body, which he's giving away freely, knowing full well the effect it'll have across our feeds. As his caption suggests, there was an egging on here, a wish for us to follow him from the dressing room onto the stage where, in characteristic fashion, Ricky would play the role of the swoon-worthy crooner he's long nurtured. Dressed in all black, with a plunging neckline that hinted at those pecs he'd showcased on his Instagram, he sang "Recuerdo" (with Carla Morrison, in all white) and "Tiburones" on an empty stage where his whispered lyrics better echoed from that audience-less pandemic awards show into our living rooms. Away from the image of the fiery, gyrating "Livin' la Vida Loca" Ricky many fans around the world still picture him as, this stripped-down (pun intended) version of Ricky is one that's both novel and strangely familiar to those of us who grew up with him as a boy-band member, as a telenovela star, and yes, as a solo artist whose ballads made our teenage selves blush.

As my share of that Ricky pic suggests ("You're welcome," I added cheekily, acknowledging how much of a gift this was to my own followers), I am somewhat obsessed with Ricky's playful forays into thirst-trap territory. This somewhat recent phenomenon feels decidedly different than the sexualized imagery that first structured his crossover success at the turn of the century. It may serve the same purpose, but the agency here strikes me as novel. His "Livin' la Vida Loca" era seemed designed to box him into the role of a fiery, excitable young man. Articles at the time kept running out of ways of telling us he was "muy caliente," playing into every stereotype about what a Puerto Rican superstar could and should be. Moreover, while his Y2K aesthetic was all coy smiles (directed, if not exclusively then implicitly, at women), his winking thirst traps feel all the more revealing. These images, disseminated through social media, get at the way we've come to commodify our bodies in virtual spaces, as well as the rippled effects they have across the web.

The linguistic acrobatics at work, carefully fine-tuned in the past few decades, are a thing of beauty. To call an image of yourself that is erotically suggestive—never explicit; you can't bait with what you freely give away, only with what you withhold—a *trap* is the kind of delicious wordplay I live for. And then there's *thirst*. As euphemisms go, the idea of desire being collapsed into such a bodily function sometimes keeps me up at night. Unlike the more straightforward concept of horniness (whose own mythic visual iconography is rife for analysis), *thirst* is more visceral, a physiological need. To feel parched is to risk dehydration. You don't merely want water. You need it. Or, rather, your body needs it. To thirst after someone, it follows, means to have a similarly instinctual reflex. The desire is framed as the kind that's hard to escape and harder still to deny. Yet the agency involved in a thirst trap, then—of those who post them, of those who enjoy them—gets ever murkier when we are dealing with a public figure, like a certain Grammy-winning artist who has come to deploy them with such gusto.

As someone who's always known a world with Ricky Martin as a pop superstar (he joined the trailblazing boy band Menudo the year I was born), I was knocked sideways by that feet post when I first encountered it back on July 25, 2017. If only I could tell my thirteen-year-old self, the one who swooned over Ricky's *Vuelve* album, that his celebrity crush would be baiting his fans to imagine where his briefs had just been (where they may yet end up!) and thus picture his chiseled physique with no CK-branded underwear to get in the way. Well, he'd lose his fucking mind.

With good reason. The Ricky I'd grown up with was a tousled-haired waif of a soloist who crooned his way through my early teenage years with slow-tempo ballads. I was much too young to have experienced the frenzy that was Menudo, so it was only once the former boy-band member transitioned into telenovela stardom that he first caught my eye. As a star in 1991's *Alcanzar una estrella II*, Ricky played Pablo, a member of the fictional pop group Muñecos de papel, which served as the main storyline for the musically inclined television series. With shoulder-length hair, oversized shirts, and an eighties fashion style to match, Ricky was clearly leaving his teenybopper years behind and stepping onto more leading-man territory. To coincide with the hit TV show, Martin released his first solo album, a self-titled collection that similarly branded him as a coy lovelorn figure. His first single, "Fuego contra fuego," like "Juego de ajedrez" (which was featured in *Alcanzar una estrella II*'s soundtrack compilation), set the then-twenty-year-old singer as a soulful, romantic lead akin to contemporary acts like Luis Miguel. At age twenty-one in 1991, Luis Miguel was already releasing his eighth album, the soon-to-be-megahit *Romance*. In his own songs, Ricky was pining over new crushes or aching over lost loves. Such emotional excess was a hallmark of his early work, and every new song released built on these kinds of lovesick narratives.

Ricky's music constantly asked him to bare his soul with emotionally raw lyrics. In "A medio vivir" he's calling up an ex to tell them how much he still misses them, how much his life now feels half-lived. In "Volverás" he regrets losing someone he loved more than he loved himself. In "Te extraño, te olvido, te amo" he bemoans how little his lover prepared him to bid them goodbye, acknowledging he's lost his sense of self entirely since they left. Even in the slightly more up-tempo "Me amarás" he sounds desperate as he promises (threatens?) his interlocutor that they *will* love him—even if he has to humiliate himself and exhaust them in turn.

It wasn't just his twinkling keyboard sound, ready-made for Friday night ugly-crying sessions. Nor his intentionally corny lyrics, which surely became fodder for plenty of breakup letters. To watch Ricky's videos from his first three solo albums is to encounter a lissome young man who was more matinee idol than hunky heartthrob. An artsy kid who'd serenade you at prom rather than the gorgeous jock who'd leave you hanging. His long flowing locks had a lot to do with this, drawing out his soft features so he looked like a beatific angel. This wasn't a hippie look nor was it a grunge one—it was much too neat and well-kept to fall into either category. But it did set him apart from those telenovela hunks whose clean-cut looks all but made them clone versions of one another. Which is all to say, early-nineties Ricky, the one I grew up with, was probably the furthest away from the swaggering, hip-swaying, thirst-trapping pop superstar we now know and love (and lust after). Witnessing this journey in real time over the past few decades has been nothing short of revolutionary, offering both a template and a warning for many of us gay boys who have grown up alongside him.

If you were to pinpoint the moment Ricky Martin's career went supernova, you'd be hard pressed to choose anything other than the evening in 1999 when he performed "The Cup of Life" at the Grammy Awards. With four albums under his belt (including the one that would net him his first Grammy win that night), Ricky wasn't an unknown. *Vuelve* had spent twenty-six weeks atop the Billboard Top Latin Albums chart, while his previous efforts had already earned him millions of fans around the world. But to a certain segment of the population—those who wouldn't know Menudo from New Kids on the Block, who maybe hadn't caught his stint on *General Hospital* let alone his leading role on *Alcanzar una estrella II* or even witnessed his talents on Broadway in *Les Misérables*—Ricky was a novel proposition. That would change overnight. By the time Madonna was congratulating him for his win, it seemed Ricky Martin would soon become a household name; "Livin' la Vida Loca" would make sure of that swiftly thereafter.

The magnetism that transfixed the Grammys audience that night wasn't new to me. I'd been finding it in smaller moments for years. An implausible hip thrust in the video for his Spanish-language take on *Hercules*'s "Go the Distance" (as he sang "Una vez te vi, era todo irreal": "Once I saw you, it was all unreal," no less!), for instance, had been intoxicating when I first caught it. Even now, when I rewatch that moment (at the 1:40 mark if you must fact-check me), I wonder if anyone else was equally as attentive to Ricky's crotch movements in the middle of Disney-produced music videos as I was back then. At a time when the thought of having openly gay singers to admire and lust after was but a farfetched fantasy, Ricky felt like the closest I could get to exploring, in silence and in secret, what I craved. Part of it had to do with the inoffensive and puppy-eyed persona he projected. Amid a myriad of male artists who exuded sanctioned predatory seduction as their de facto sensibility, Ricky was a welcome balm, a soft and soft-spoken singer whose coyness was part of his persona.

Even in a song like "María," where his lyrics obviously put him in conversation with a woman, the video for the song kept him respectfully walled off from such opposite-sex pairings. In the original video, shot at a concert in Argentina, you mostly see Ricky singing onstage and in the middle of a street, with nary a romantic subplot to be found. And in the Paris-shot version, released once the 1995 remix took off in Europe, you again see just Ricky, dancing in the French capital. Only, in this version (which is the one the artist now showcases on his YouTube page), you see glimpses of women. They dance in the streets. They're riding in a car. They're lounging in bed. But their connection with Ricky remains diffuse. Are they memories of the María he's singing about? Former paramours who still tug at his heartstrings? It's unclear. They feel rather like afterthoughts in the video itself, not least because they never share screen time with the singer. It's as if viewers were being called to suture these images—of the pretty boy on the streets and the girl in the sheets—to dream up the heterosexual pairing the song begged for.

No other music video from this era, though, better captures why Ricky so spoke to me as both masculine role model and budding gay crush than "Vuelve." Watching that video, off of his same-titled 1998 album, was to come the closest to firmly asking myself: Do I want him or do I just want to be him?

In "Vuelve," Ricky is effortlessly cool. Not cool as in aloof and detached, donning sunglasses and sitting at the back of the class. Cool as in you wish you could pull off wearing a pair of athleisure pants and a tight-fitted see-through sweater with such ease. As he sings about the love he's lost and hopes will return (ergo the title of the song), Ricky mostly stands around the Ennis House in Los Angeles, letting the Mayan-inspired stonework on the walls better show off his frame— and his beautiful, clean-shaven face (seriously, his dewy complexion and perfectly tousled hair are almost unbearable to look at). Add that he's wearing no shoes and no socks and you have a kind of imag- ined intimacy. (There is something intrinsically erotic, I find, about bare feet; it's perhaps why that rainbow-hued Insta pic so tickled me, reminding me of his most soulful video.) Here was Ricky at his most vulnerable, his image a carefully curated set of signifiers that marked him as a hopeless romantic. As the lyrics suggested, he was an open wound. Here was a man at peace with his own emotions, unafraid to let such emotional excess be released out into the world.

"Kiki," as he was known to those closest to him, had a softness that was both enviable and seductive. Even when I didn't know Ricky would one day come out publicly, I understood something about the graceful masculinity he projected. There was a tenderness I gravitated toward. A coziness about his soft pliability that felt infinitely preferable to the gruff (at best) and oppressive (at worst) images of ruggedly handsome men I was encouraged to identify with and never dare covet.

This would all change with "Livin' la Vida Loca." The first single from his self-titled English-language debut album built on the booming, dance-ready sounds he'd flirted with in "La copa de la vida" (Draco Rosa and Desmond Child wrote and produced both tracks). Gone was the coyness, the looks askance, and the heartrending lyrics. In came a fiery explosion of sounds and sex appeal. It's there in the blaring horns, yes, and the thumping bass. And in the swagger of a song Rosa and Child conceived for a kind of "Latin Elvis" with a Rat Pack sound that would borrow heavily from The Doors and Jim Morrison. But it's most noticeable in the music video that accompanies this absolute banger of a hit.

Directed by Wayne Isham, the video kicks off with an image as euphemistic of male bravado as you can muster: a car skids across a corner and hits a fire hydrant that's about to gush all its contents across the screen. Only the shot cuts before such an image can wash over us. It's the horns that take over the screen instead, Ricky's band ushering us into a feverish late-night-out scenario. Don't worry, though: we return to the geyser that comes from the fire hydrant minutes later. Its explosion, and the dancers it drenches in turn, stand in for the song's

orgiastic pleasures. Playfully echoing the song's lyrics, the video in-
troduces Ricky as bewitched by the kind of crazed and crazy woman
he sings about (remember, she's a woman who's as likely to ask you to
take off your clothes and go dancing in the rain as she is to take your
pain away like a bullet to your brain). In the role of this sexy mysteri-
ous gal is Croatian model Nina Morić, who spends most of the video
in a skimpy strapless number trying to get Ricky to pay attention to
her while they drive around at night. And while he steals a glance here
or there, there's no denying he's a responsible driver; he continues to
stare ahead even when she's eager to straddle him. She's enamored
with this man, losing any and all sense of propriety.

This was the Ricky packaged for the MTV crowd. The one who
flustered even Rosie O'Donnell during his Grammy awards performance. The one who would be named one of *People* magazine's sexiest
men alive and who would be dubbed a Latin heartthrob by every publication that fawned over the music industry's latest "find." More egre-
gious still was "She Bangs," the first single from his quickly released
follow-up album. Not only did the lyrics now explicitly conjure up an
explosive sexual encounter (he notes he'll let her rough him up) but its
accompanying video felt like a straight man's fever dream. Set at a hidden underwater club of sorts (don't ask), Ricky finds himself dancing
for everyone to admire. In the most infamous shot of the video, Ricky
is lying down, his unbuttoned white shirt billowing around him the
better to show off his well-defined abs. His distressed denim pants are
unbuttoned (of course) as various naked figures writhe below him,
with many a hand groping his torso as he thrashes in ecstasy. Where
"Livin' la Vida Loca" suggested a sex craze, "She Bangs" literalized it.

I've long been curious about this crossover reinvention. It didn't
feel particularly performative—or, rather, not more performative than
the onstage personas of his contemporaries, all of whom trafficked
in exaggerated versions of their oversexualized personalities. For all
I knew, Ricky wanted to move away from his soulful ballads, having

found global success with more upbeat songs like "María" (*the* ines-capable ear worm of 1995 . . . and 1996, 1997, and 1998; that's how ubiquitous it was with every subsequent CD rerelease). But it did feel like there was a push to transition Ricky when he began singing in English. There was his hair, for starters, which was nicely cropped and colored (no more mop-headed teen heartthrob there); in fact, in a magazine article I am now convinced I dreamed up, I remember reading a breakdown of Ricky's hair that argued that the rest of us guys should take note: the bulkier the singer got, the shorter his hair was cut. This was in keeping with how we were to think of our hair-styles, long locks seemingly being better suited to waiflike bodies, while buzzcuts and the like were, apparently, de rigueur if you had muscles to show off. I imagine it had something to do with wanting to keep some semblance of balance. The commentary has stayed with me since, mostly because it used the singer('s body) as a template the rest of us were supposed to follow.

When Ricky finally came out publicly in 2010 ahead of releas-ing his memoir (a perfect a collision of public and private, marketing and self-reflection), I devoured it, hoping to find insights into how the singer felt about that time in his life. Unsurprisingly, though, the bluntly titled *Me* offered little in the way of such introspection. The memoir was mostly a compilation of empty platitudes ("Life is a jour-ney and every step we take moves us in some direction"; "All of my joys and pains have made me who I am."), but it did sometimes, al-most unintentionally, express illuminating insights.

As a storyteller, Ricky is comically oblique. At the start of the book he notes he'll be omitting certain details so as to maintain a sense of privacy both for himself and those in his life. The result is a number of anecdotes stripped of any specificity, with his inner strug-gles sketched out in general terms that end up reading like a rather bland version of self-help: "I believe that everything that happens in life happens for a reason," he earnestly repeats over and over as he takes readers from Puerto Rico to New York to Mexico City to Los Angeles and beyond, with nary a snippet of in-the-moment insights. Romances get flattened into meet-cutes that turn into breakups. Record deals get collapsed into "sign here" vignettes. Even a hectic journey to San Remo that involves a car crash is telegraphed with such blunt efficiency that it's clear Ricky isn't interested in crafting scenes, just lessons. The memoir is, in a way, an exercise in evasion. Or, rather, in careful curation. Just as young Ricky, as he slowly reveals, dove headfirst into tireless work (as a member of Menudo, as a telenovela star, as a solo singer, as a crossover artist) and into oft-hollow relationships (mostly with women, but also in secret with various men) so as to avoid grappling with his sexuality, the memoir dances around fascinating thematic threads as it trudges along toward this notion that everything happens when it's supposed to. Which is to say, his belated coming out was less a story of long-running struggle than one of waiting for the stars to align for him to best find the strength to know himself and share (however evasively) that truth with the world.

But it's clear, even in his choice to publish his memoir (in both English and Spanish, no less), that Ricky wanted to exorcize some of the demons he'd been wrestling with for decades, in the hope, perhaps, that others would find something to learn from his journey. Early in *Me*, Ricky articulates a recurring theme in his life and that of many young boys, Latino or otherwise, who have to navigate their every preference as a sign of their masculinity. "Despite the fact that the boys from Menudo were my idols," he remembers, "and I yearned to be a part of the group, for the majority of kids my age Menudo was a girl thing. Culturally and socially, we were so conditioned—in part due to ignorance and in part to envy—to think that real men don't like to sing and dance, that for a kid like me to want to do it was considered ridiculous." As the sole male soprano in our school choir (there were only three boys total), I weathered my fair share of insults rooted in similar conditioning. During every school assembly performance (a Beatles song here, a Christmas medley there; the national anthem here, a chorus-heavy number from the school's musical there), I could feel the snickers coming from my classmates. Their mocking glances pierced right through me and caused me to blush in shame, forced as I was to see myself through their eyes. And find in them a degree of recognition. For I did enjoy things that I was taught and told were "for girls." Not just choir practice and musicals and telenovelas but, more crucially, the longing for the comfort of men.

If Ricky is particularly eloquent about the push and pull of conforming to culturally ingrained ideals of masculinity while growing up, he's less so when it comes to examining how he grappled with it as a twentysomething performer who was thrust into the highest echelons of global fame and had to contend with an at-times tone-deaf press corps that couldn't wait to box him into a neatly packaged persona. Indeed, coverage of Ricky following that Grammy performance is comically revealing. Take the 1999 cover story for *Time* magazine ("Latin music goes POP!"), which begins with a description of a throng of screaming fans outside a Tower Records store in Manhattan ("Mostly sopranos and altos, a few tenors and no basses.") before the scene is pit against early screenings of *Star Wars: Episode I – The Phantom Menace* happening across the street. The fangirl and the fanboy are intentionally framed as incongruous and diametrically opposed camps. *Time* goes on to argue that Ricky was but the prime example of a new generation of Latin acts sweeping the nation's airwaves yet again (Gloria Estefan had paved the way but fifteen years earlier). But, as the Shakira crossover that would follow, the "Despacito" craze that came about a decade later, and Bad Bunny's eventual streaming dominance illustrate, Latine and Latin American artists seem to always be in a Sisyphean cycle of constantly exploding in the U.S. market— and constantly being reductively talked about in mainstream media. Ricky arrived at just the right time.

Like *Time*, *The New York Times* continually tripped over itself trying to explain Ricky in terms of his Latinidad. After his Grammy Awards performance, Peter Watrous wrote, "He has become a symbol on two sexy feet of Latin culture's new mainstream status in the United States." The next paragraph unironically goes on to list how his "Latino credentials are in order," pointing out that he's "originally from Puerto Rico" and also "a United States citizen" who speaks English. This is but a small example of how little cultural intelligibility the vexing concept of Latinidad had in mainstream U.S. media. It's no surprise Ricky spends some time recounting these experiences in *Me* in ways that further distance him from such reductive labels. Noting how the press in the United States so quickly dubbed him a "Latin act" after he'd been an "international artist" all over the world, was but one way in which Ricky realized that "many Americans, perhaps the majority, know very little about Latin culture," adding that "their knowledge is often based on a number of prejudices and preconceptions that are completely wrong."

One of those major prejudices and preconceptions was squarely centered on the figure of the "Latin lover": "I think that one of the reasons why I found it so hard to accept myself," he writes in *Me*, "was because in my profession I have often been considered to be a Latin idol, a pop star, and for some, a sex symbol. I don't know if it has to do with the fact that I am Latin or if it has to do with the global image of the 'Latin lover,' but I always had the feeling that certain things were expected of me, among which was the fact that I was supposed to seduce—and allow myself to be seduced by—women." He may not call them out by name, but images of "Livin' la Vida Loca" and "She Bangs" were instrumental in upholding those expectations.

For all his protestations decades after the fact, Ricky's packaging as a Latin heartthrob felt, to many of us back then, as shamelessly intentional. Again, one need only look at that "She Bangs" video or the similarly themed *Rolling Stone* cover image from August 1999 where, dressed in all white (yet carefully showing off his abs despite wearing a

tank top, a billowy white shirt, and white pants), Ricky is surrounded
by naked women in a sky-blue pool. Shot by queer photographer
David LaChapelle, known for his hyperrealistic kitschy sensibility,
the image yet again positioned Ricky as a male hunk right at home
in selling his image to those eager to consume him. Funnily enough,
even as the final image chosen for the cover finds the artist smiling,
euphorically taking the scene in great stride, an alternate version offers a decidedly different scenario. The shot is basically the same; only
Ricky's expression is changed. He's still smiling but almost through
gritted teeth, begging us to ask how he ended up surrounded by all
those naked women in the first place.

I recognize that expression all too well. It's not so much a cry for
help as a naked commentary on the absurdity of what you're being
asked to endorse. Not quite "Yikes! Why are all these girls naked,
drowning themselves all around me as I call out for help to someone
above?" but also not *not* that. The gap between those two photographs
may well be the schism that existed between Kiki and Ricky. Between
who Ricky was and who he was called to be. Or, perhaps more accurately, between the Ricky he knew himself to be and the one he hoped
he could become. As a kid, he'd lied to his schoolmates and told them
he wanted to join Menudo for the girls; here he was practicing yet another lie of omission. Ricky, as in every other public appearance, looks
exquisitely well-put-together (his lips plump and red, his teeth impossibly white, his hair beautifully coiffed and highlighted), though
actually quite delicate—a vulnerable stud if there ever was one. Ricky
spoke to me because he seemed to embody these various contradictions, as if under the surface I could already glimpse the cracks of
that packaged version of masculinity he was constantly called upon to
perform. Looking at these paired images I can't help but project onto
them the insecurities I grew up with in Colombia, where I had a hard
time squaring my more effeminate proclivities with the push to feel
at home in spaces that so obviously demeaned women for my benefit.

On May 8, 1999, three days before his self-titled English-language album was released, Ricky Martin appeared as the musical guest on *Saturday Night Live* in an episode hosted by Cuba Gooding Jr. Visually echoing the video for his hit single (then the number one song in the United States), Ricky's performance was all gyrating hips and scantily clad female backup dancers. Wearing his then-signature combo of tightly fitted thin knitwear up top and leather pants down below, he was a ball of energy, exuding the sex appeal he sang about. A year later, when Ricky would return to the show to promote his hastily produced album *Sound Loaded*, cast member Chris Kattan would take the chance to preface the singer's performance by openly mimicking and mocking Ricky and his moves. With an unbuttoned shirt and a series of spastic arm and hip gestures, Kattan turned Ricky into a walking stereotype, all before the real Ricky stepped onto the stage and ushered him away with a bashful laugh, telling him and audience alike that such dances (to the tune of "Livin' la Vida Loca") were already old news. He was there to promote his new album and its single, "Loaded," which not only implores listeners to walk like a "loaded man" but to swing "like a thong."

It was Kattan who had also pulled focus in that earlier 1999 Gooding Jr. episode with an infamous sketch where he reprised one of his most well-known characters: the swishy, gold-sequin-shorts-wearing Mango. If Ricky's dancing and demeanor were aggressively coded as heterosexual, as if to ward off the whispers that would soon follow him, the Mango sketch Kattan performed with Gooding Jr. offered its inverse. Mango was a lisping exotic dancer who captivated all who encountered him. Over the years, the effeminate, vaguely Latino-coded character had unwittingly seduced the likes of David Duchovny and Garth Brooks. In the sketch with Gooding Jr.—which features the Oscar winner flashing his ass at Kattan in an attempt to woo the coy Mango—we get to meet Mango's family. Much to the shock of Gooding Jr. (and the audience), Mango is happily married to a woman (played by Molly Shannon); therein lay the punchline. He's also the father of two kids: a young boy who looks just like him, curved sideburns and all, and a baby his wife holds throughout the sketch in their dull suburban living room. Taken together, especially in such proximity to one another, there's no way to avoid seeing Ricky and Mango as capturing two sides of the same coin, twinned pop culture images that trafficked on that alluring figure: the "Latin lover." The comedy Kattan and the *SNL* writers wrung out of grounding Mango's flamboyance in a straight marriage, confounding the effeminate markers that nevertheless seduced every straight male host that came near him, was merely an aggrandized version of what Ricky himself projected.

"I believe one of the factors that contributed to the rumors about my sexuality was that people maybe thought my image as the 'Latin lover' was excessive," he writes in *Me*, "perhaps they thought that everything I did—the way I danced, the lyrics to my songs, my sexy onstage moves—was nothing but an attempt to conceal my homosexuality." But therein lay the crux of this whole affair. From its origins on the big screen, courtesy of Rudolph Valentino, the Latin lover has always been defined by an excess of *both* masculinity and femininity. As Brian Eugenio Herrera, author of *Latin Numbers: Playing Latino in Twentieth-Century U.S. Popular Performance*, puts it, "His thrilling, romantic, flouncing flourish conceals the threat of the rapacious, forceful libido." He is both too macho and too feminine. This was the comedy in Mango: no matter how ridiculously effeminate you thought he was (what with his tiny berets and gyrating, lisping ways), he was still irrepressibly seductive. Yet, and here's what the Cuba Gooding Jr. sketch further hammered home, he was a breadwinner, a husband, and a father, a monogamous one at that. He may have kept the libido he inspired in others in check, but it was the laughter Kattan elicited out of his signature catchphrase ("You can't have the Mango!") that truly neutralized the effect he had on those around him.

Explaining the origins of Mango, Kattan inadvertently reveals what makes this beloved (and, it must be noted, hilarious) character such a curious provocation. When coming up with Mango, who is named after a real-life stripper he'd once seen perform, the comedian drew from two incongruent but complementary inspirations: a Russian ex-girlfriend who, when mad, would volley a cutesy response like "I kill you, Kattan!" with a sly pout, and his Dalmatian, Lola, who, when called, would coyly look back and swish her butt at him. It's no accident that Mango would be based in part on a woman; his is a glittering, fabulous energy that feels very feminine. It helps that he often wore sequins and skirts. Foreignness, too, was integral to what made Mango such a funny character. That, and the arched self-awareness that characterized his sketches. In a 2001 appearance with Jennifer Lopez, where Mango becomes a recording artist, he gets called out for shopping at the women's section after he and Lopez arrive wearing the same outfit. "This is a men's cut!" he protests, "Why does everybody think I'm the homo-gay? WHY?! WHY?! WHY?!" he dramatically wails, before offering the requisite deadpan punchline in his lisping accent: "Maybe I know why."

Such a character helped further the anxieties Ricky experienced firsthand—this sense that foreign masculinities were cast as too effeminate on the one hand and yet aggressively heterosexual on the other. Seduction, as the "Latin lover" trope tells us, comes from an odd allegiance between tenderness and danger, between softness and aggression. It's no surprise Ricky distanced himself from such strictures even decades after the fact, especially since his every move (whether a hip thrust here or a coy smirk there) was constantly policed and used to discern whether he was the womanizing heartthrob his songs boasted he was or, God forbid, the loose-limbed closeted gay man others worried he was.

It's ridiculous to presume to know what a person's Instagram feed says about them. Curation is an invisible skill; we only ever see part of the story. Yet to browse Ricky's many thot-full Instagram posts of late—here a perfectly framed out-of-the-shower shot, there a poolside photo with his artist husband, Jwan Yosef—is to see someone that "Livin' la Vida Loca"–era Ricky couldn't have fathomed. Or, and here I can be more authoritative about it, I can't help but see someone my teenage self could never have anticipated. There's an unguarded sexiness about Ricky at fifty, which feels not so much like a corrective to that carefully curated image of the Latin lover as much as a necessary expansion of it. When I see him teasing a new song and video with a photo of him in a bathtub, his eyes gazing off frame as water droplets adorn his sun-tanned torso, or a post where he shares a magazine cover image where he stands shirtless while being cradled by Jwan, the two men caught in a beautifully intimate hug for *CAP 74024*'s 2021 Pride issue (shot by Matthew Brookes), I see a man at ease with himself, who is all too happy to offer himself to us unfiltered. Or, as unfiltered as such painstakingly curated images will allow.

And yet, as his social media presence suggests, such forays into thirst-trap territory have come with undue consequences. That latter image, which openly celebrated his relationship with Jwan and presented a tender moment between two shirtless (heck, maybe even naked; the shot cuts them off at the nipples) men provoked a slew of homophobic and retrograde comments—and, to hear Martin talk about it in a follow-up post, a significant loss in followers.

He'd earned similarly intolerant comments a few weeks before when he'd shared another magazine editorial (this time for *Schön!* magazine, shot by Isaac Anthony). Where the styling for *CAP 74024* kept Ricky and Jwan in conversation with postwar images of masculinity (white tees and dark jeans, leather jackets and harnesses), their ruggedly handsome faces lovingly juxtaposed with their heart-tugging, swoon-worthy poses, the *Schön!* shoot placed Martin in decidedly different territory. Sporting his pandemic bleach-blond beard as well as more outré fashion, the photographs selected for the two digital covers captured a side of Ricky he had rarely indulged in. In one, wearing a pair of high-waisted unbuttoned denim pants and a leather halter top, Ricky is squatting, showing off the black heeled boots he's wearing. His bulked-up muscles are front and center; his arm is resting on his knee, his wrist limply hovering in the air ("Is he . . . you know?" I muse to myself) while his fixed gaze seems to be calling to us. There's a resigned confrontation to pose and photo alike, as if Ricky were unwittingly daring us to say anything about him. In the other, his expression is more legible. Seated, legs wide open in matching leather jacket and pants with a mesh T-shirt underneath, a cigarette between his nail-polished hands, his come hither look is unmissable. His closed lips, framed by his primly trimmed blond beard, beckon us. He looks both imperious and inviting.

It's clear why some would have balked at these pictures, some presenting a normalized image of same-sex desire, the others a defiant vision of queered fashion. When he'd sung about shaking his bonbon and livin' la vida loca, his sexualized persona had been celebrated; his body was then a legible trope sold on magazine covers. Two decades (and a coming out) later, you'd think his decision to sexualize himself and to weaponize his body to uplift his love for his husband (or his love of fabulous fashion and glitter as one other *Schön!* photo finds him doing, throwing a golden fistful of it in the air, catching it with his bare torso) would be moot. Yet the discomfort that led (and still leads) so many, albeit a minority, to comment hateful things under these types of pictures ("Muy grotesco," "No disimula lo que le gusta," followed by puking emojis) shows how destabilizing such images continue to be, images where a man is seen embracing aspects of himself he's been told to neglect, to ignore, to hide, to suppress. To push back on the hateful messages he'd received when he shared those *CAP 74024* pictures with his husband, Martin posted a long screed that outlined his disappointment at such blowback: "Lo más que deseo en esta vida es que todos podamos sentirnos libres, orgullosos de nosotros mismos, felices, que seamos amados, respetados y aceptados," he wrote (just in Spanish, though he often offers bilingual captions, in itself an indication of which audience he most hoped would read this message), "Que podamos expresarnos cómo nos nace sin tener represalias o ser castigados." What he most wishes is that we could all feel free and proud of ourselves, happy and loved and respected and accepted. That we could express ourselves however we wished without fear of being punished.

His choice of image was, given his rhetoric, all the more telling. Donning a simple black T-shirt, the photos (by Alejandro Pedrosa) found the singer showing off a set of long and colorful acrylic nails. Called to perform a version of himself neutered of homosexuality and femininity, the two so wholly intertwined in our cultural imagination (Why can't he just shake his bonbon for his adoring female fans like he used to? Why must he choose to so sully his image like this nowadays?), Ricky's subtle fuck you, simple and cutting as it may appear, shows us a man finally at home in his own body, in his own masculinity, eager to not restrict it to what's long been demanded of him and hopeful instead of what doors it may yet open for others in his wake.

7.

Laws of Desire

THERE IS NOTHING SEXIER THAN A MAN IN A PAIR OF WHITE briefs.

I must admit their appeal comes from their ubiquity. Boxers with hearts on them may have been the go-to imagery for Saturday morning cartoons and modest boxer briefs may have been all the rage in Abercrombie & Fitch advertisements. But there's no denying that the simple and pure and therefore unassuming Y-front white brief stands as the industry standard when any one of us wants to dream up the ideal for men's underwear.

But maybe I should only speak for myself. I find briefs enticing for what they do to the male body. Unlike other types of underwear—say, boxer briefs, whose rise in popularity very much coincided with my teenage years—briefs have the perfect thigh-to-bulge ratio. Boxers hide and thongs flaunt, but briefs titillate by the very shape they contour and convey. Furry thighs and fuzzy navels create a landscape worth exploring, rolling hills that entice those eager to go sightseeing down below. As utilitarian as they may be, briefs have a way of coyly suggesting that which garments like jockstraps (and yes, wrestling singlets) handsomely outline. Plus, unlike athletic gear, briefs have a welcome mundanity to them. They're tied to a bland ideal of masculinity that they eroticize in delightfully unintentional ways.

Moreover, there's something bashful about a man wearing nothing but briefs. That's why its arrival in advertising campaigns in the 1980s was greeted with such breathless adulation. For, if we are to trust *American Photographer* magazine, there was a day in 1982 when "the world awoke to find that sex had changed." This was two years before I was born, so in cases like these, I'm stuck trusting the truthfulness of such a hyperbolic pronouncement if not, perhaps, its accuracy. It was that year that Calvin Klein launched what would become one of the most successful ad campaigns of all time, plastering a sun-licked picture of Olympic pole vaulter Tom Hintnaus on a forty-five-foot Times Square billboard. The Bruce Weber photograph, which featured Hintnaus languidly leaning against a bleach-white wall in Santorini, his bulge front and center in a pair of Calvin Klein's signature white briefs, shocked many a bystander, causing a flurry of controversy that paved the way for the decades-long run of CK ads featuring beautiful male models in little else than tight-fitting, branded underwear. With his eyes closed, Hintnaus's tanned body did most of the communicating. As curator Diana Edkins told *American Photographer* in their "10 Pictures That Changed America" feature, "It was the height, the epitome of a sexual liberation, primarily for men," adding that the photo "changed what advertising could be and could show from then on."

What could be shown was, of course, a man in his underwear. In briefs, no less. This was, at the time, revelatory in all senses of the word. Hintnaus's body was an instrument that had, for years, been scrupulously examined by sports commentators, Olympic officials, and fans alike, and was here seen in repose. Presented for our consumption so as to encourage a decidedly different kind of consumption. No longer would this be the sole realm of female models. Men could just as easily be dangled in front of our eyes.

The Hintnaus photo felt in line with the envelope-pushing advertising ethos of the famed denim brand. In 1980, the designer had enlisted a then-fifteen-year-old Brooke Shields for what would become a controversial (and thus instantly iconic) TV ad where the actress would ask the camera, "Do you wanna know what comes between me and my Calvins?" only to offer as tantalizing an answer as you can imagine: "Nothing." The hint of the erotic (Shields was wearing a pair of jeans and a beige shirt; she couldn't have been *more* covered up) was what's long been at the core of Calvin Klein's campaigns. As Marc Jacobs put it in a conversation with Klein for *Interview* magazine in 2013, "Calvin's clothing seemed to be all about the sensation of touch," later telling his fellow designer, "With you, it was more about an aesthetic, the dream of this beauty—those bodies, those faces." He may at first have been selling clothing, but above all Klein was always selling a lifestyle, one built upon, as Jacobs put it, "the provocation of getting naked."

The CK image of a blissful man in his briefs is but one example of how the 1980s turned that seemingly basic undergarment into a sexy prop. Originally designed in the 1930s as an offshoot of the jockstrap, boasting the same, ahem, support but with a European twist (inspired, as lore has it, by a postcard from the French Riviera picturing a man wearing a tight-fitting swimsuit), these "Jockeys" went from hot new item to run-of-the-mill apparel in the decades that followed. Hollywood, though, opted for years to still feature the reliable pair of boxers lest those thighs (and bulges) make their films look racier than they'd otherwise be. That is until the briefs went mainstream in the 1980s. One need only think of Tom Cruise dancing in his tighty-whities in *Risky Business*. Of Keanu Reeves shaking his "cute butt" in *Parenthood* in similar attire. Of Christian Bale showing off his physique at the start of the 1987-set film *American Psycho*. And yes, of Marty McFly in *Back to the Future* having to take on the moniker of Calvin Klein once his mom (a teenager in the past Marty has time-traveled to) peeks at the branded briefs he's wearing and assumes he's personalized his undergarments. Or, if we travel farther out, away from the United States, Gael García Bernal diving into a pool in his white, soon-to-be-see-through briefs in an imagined version of 1980 Madrid in 2004's *La mala educación*.

As someone who spent an inordinate amount of time in the underwear aisle at our local department store when in need of a new pair (or three), I can't thank Klein enough. Underwear models were some of my earliest memories of seeing the male body so displayed; here you were encouraged to take them in. To see how tight (or loose) they fit. See how far up they ran or how low they hung. The, uh, briefs, I mean. I didn't encounter the Hintnaus photo until years after it had changed sex forever (whatever that meant); I was more likely to have first encountered CK ads by way of Marky Mark and his cheeky boxer brief photos (by Herb Ritts), replete with his hand grabbing his junk in mock defiance of whoever was on the other end of his gaze.

But the subtle (homo)eroticism that has come to define the CK brand since (one need only peruse the MyCalvins hashtag on Instagram) was there in Weber's original campaign. As Klein shared with Jacobs, that shoot was meant to introduce their underwear line, "and it was about the body. When the face was turned away, it was always about the body. But then sex always came right back into it. You know, I collect antiquities." That non sequitur connecting antiquities to the toned bodies of the models Klein initially handpicked himself (to hear him tell it, he found Hintnaus while driving down Sunset Boulevard, was struck dumb by his beauty, and signed him all but on the spot) is telling. Classical antiquity–era busts and torsos, the kind displayed in art museums all over the world, are some of the most socially sanctioned examples of the male form's beauty. They were the only other instances where, in public, I was asked to gaze at the male body undressed. And yes, sex always hovered ever out of frame.

On that note I should probably amend my earlier statement. For whenever I think of a man in a pair of white briefs it is not Hintnaus I picture. Nor is it myself (though that kind of narcissism has come into play the more pieces of underwear I've come to accumulate over the years). No, I'm always thinking of a certain Pedro Almodóvar muse. For there is nothing sexier than Antonio Banderas in a pair of white briefs.

If such an image eludes you, I hope it's because you've not yet had the pleasure of watching the Spanish filmmaker's 1987 queer neo-noir *La ley del deseo* (*Law of Desire*). I've long held that all you need to know in life you can learn from Almodóvar's Oscar-winning film, *Todo sobre mi madre* (*All About My Mother*), but it is his earlier flick that I find most instructive when I think of my queer upbringing. I sometimes mourn the gay man I could be now if I'd found this outré riff on a Patricia Highsmith plot earlier in my life. Earlier that is, than when I was in my early twenties and first found out (from a gobsmacked friend!) that Almodóvar was gay, a detail I clearly must have missed, or more likely ignored, when his films were promoted in Colombia in my teens. But then I console myself by remembering that it is never too late to luxuriate in the ways of Almodóvar. I should be happy I ever found him at all. For in finding him I encountered a kindred spirit. Perhaps not someone I wanted to be or become, but someone who seemed keyed into my same wavelength. Someone whose love of melodrama led him to create some of the most fascinating and complicated women I'd ever seen on the big screen, and whose love of men led him to conjure up some of the most delectable male characters I've encountered. Delectable but also, the more I've spent time with them over the years, despicable. And deplorable. And disreputable. Not that the women in his films are all blushing flowers or saintly martyrs. But there's something to be said about the joy the filmmaker has taken in creating male characters who are as likely to seduce you as they are to kill you. None exemplify this better than Banderas's Antonio in *La ley del deseo*, a character and performance that capture the undeniable erotic charisma that thereafter made the Spanish actor the go-to guy for any (and all) Hollywood roles that called for a "Latin lover" type. It's easily one of the Almodóvar films I've rewatched the most in my lifetime (give or take its spiritual sibling, *La mala educación*, which has always felt to me like a twisted remake of this earlier Antonio vehicle). *La ley del deseo* is a film I return to time and time again to find new angles to what's ostensibly a delirious exploration of the rote allure of masculinity and the self-destructive power of same-sex desire.

When I first saw *La ley del deseo* on my laptop, holed away in my dorm room, I remember having to pause it not even ten minutes in. Here was a movie that outright scandalized me. Not because it showed things I didn't want to see, but because it so flagrantly flaunted that which I desperately craved to watch. Its first scene begins with a young man undressing for an unseen interlocutor who demands he strip down. Only, such a demand is not enough. The disembodied voice later asks him to stare at his reflection. To kiss himself there. To rub himself against the mirror and later still, to lose his white briefs altogether and pretend he's being fucked while on all fours on a bed, all while vocalizing what he wants done to himself. "Fóllame!" he's instructed to moan: "Fuck me!"

Just describing it makes me blush.

It wasn't that there was anything particularly pornographic about it—though, yes, there's the sense that this could very well be one of the many gay-for-pay porn videos I've clicked on in the years since, where the prospect of a straight, or straight-seeming, dude is egged on to debase himself for the benefit of unseen spectators, us included. It's that the scene assaults you so wholly as if defying you to look away. Here was a fantasy I'd long toyed with, one that I spent years tending to. I still remember how in the locker room at my local gym, where for two months I convinced myself I could begin toning my sixteen-year-old ropy body (I didn't; I've yet to find the discipline for it even all these decades later), I ached for a glimpse of a fellow gym-goer in just his underwear. I didn't dare imagine more. For the longest time, in fact, I dabbled in forums where gay porn stories were bountiful (many, now that I think about them, centered on strippers). I preferred the fantasies I could picture in my mind to the ones pornography so nakedly offered up online. Naked men for my perusing pleasure were, presumably, always a click away, but in the digital jungle that was the Web 1.0, I often found myself fending off malware viruses and an exponential explosion of pop-up ads that made the low-quality JPEGs (or, on rare occasions, the pixelated, always buffering MP4s) not worth the trouble. Moreover, it was always much more titillating to dream up what lay underneath ("Is not the most erotic portion of a body where the garment gapes?" as Roland Barthes puts it) than to try to grapple with the specifics of other male bodies. It was a leap of imaginative faith that in the 1990s, amid scaremongering AIDS rhetoric, felt distinctly dangerous, even in the abstract. That was why to display yourself wearing nothing but a pair of Y-fronts, as the young man in *La ley del deseo* does, was to toy with a kind of intimacy my recently out college-aged self still couldn't yet fathom, precisely the kind I coveted.

More importantly, and obviously serving as a horny précis of the film, this prologue complicates the question of who is in control of this lustful image: Is it the young hustler as he caresses his body, his briefs, his bulge? Or is he merely a puppet for whoever's barking orders off camera, a mere object to be bossed around for our own benefit? Might this pliable young stud offer us some insight into how men eroticize their own bodies for other men? It's hard not to read into this transactional dynamic, where the power imbalance tilts heavily to one side, a kind of archetypal same-sex encounter in the sense that watching an unnamed trick let himself become the object of someone else's gaze, someone who may not be as attractive, as muscular, as imposing—as manly, say—feels tiredly familiar. Not just in porn scenarios (Sean Cody, anyone?) but in decades' worth of cruising anecdotes featuring faceless boys picked up at seedy rest stops or abandoned piers or late-night streets.

No other writer has so painstakingly chronicled these kinds of encounters than John Rechy, the author of the infamous *City of Night*, a thinly disguised autobiographical novel published in 1963 in which the Chicano writer sketched out the world of hustling and cruising he himself had navigated as a young man, often relishing in similar scenes wherein the hustler is wholly in control of a situation that depends on his own sexual submission. As Rechy points out time and time again, such intentional imbalances have everything to do with the fraught relationship men—however they identify—have with masculinity, their own and that of the men they cruise. As Rechy's narrator puts it in *City of Night*, masculinity was both draw and threat when it came to the men on the streets, desired and disdained often in the same breath. "From the very beginning," he writes, "I had become aware of overtones of defensive derision aimed by some scores at those young men they picked up for the very masculinity they would later disparage—as if convinced, or needfully proclaiming their conviction, that the more masculine a hustler, the more his masculinity is a subterfuge." A way to neuter (or wholly undo) such subterfuge, as Rechy's speaker finds, was for those "scores" (the men picking up young hustlers) to take pleasure in getting their tricks to submit to their own desires. To debase such a man played into a primal sexual fantasy, one that wrestled power and control from those who would otherwise best wield it.

In *The Sexual Outlaw*, Rechy's 1977 book that presented itself as a "prose documentary" that chronicled, as its tagline suggested, "three days and nights in the sexual underground," the author stages a scene not unlike the one that opens Almodóvar's *La ley del deseo*. Rechy's protagonist ("Jim"), yet another autobiographical avatar, cruises the streets even after earning success publishing scandalously racy books that glorify the lurid aspects of the gay male experience in the 1970s.

He reminisces at one point about a deliciously erotic hookup where an older man took him home, though sex was not what this other man wanted. Instead, he wanted merely to admire Jim from afar, directing his every move in front of a series of mirrors. Jim is asked to play the part of an aloof, unattainable cowboy (boots, denim shorts, and jockstrap are provided) who'll parade himself for a gawking onlooker, kneeling in adoration before him. It's an image the man is intent on recreating from one of the many pornographic magazines he has scattered all over his place. "In the mirror across the room Jim saw himself, the fantasy framed," Rechy writes, "He basked in sexual power, his power to personify the cherished fantasy in this fusing of two dreams." He's then ordered to undress, all while asked to be indifferent to his interlocutor, who narrates the entire encounter for himself: "Ignoring me and staring at himself while I stare at him, and he knows I idolize him, he knows it," the man tells Jim. The scene moves toward a sexual tableau vivant where Jim's role is merely that of a model to be looked at: "Not letting me touch it until he's ready," the man continues, "just looking in the mirror, knowing how much I want him." The pageantry of the cowboy, that role model of American masculinity, is enough to rile up desire from afar, especially when he's forced to expose himself to us, to sexualize and fetishize his own body for our viewing pleasure—it's a scene that would make Myra Breckinridge proud.

The unnamed man eventually escalates the scene by approaching Jim and sucking him off, a kind of salacious happy ending Rechy's books were full of: "In the framed mirror, Jim saw his own cum spill in slow arcking [sic] spurts as the man directed the white liquid onto his clothed body, on the jockstrap, on his face, on his lips, over the open magazine, and on the photograph in it of a muscular man standing naked over a clothed man surrounded in bed by magazines of photographs of muscular nude bodies." This kaleidoscopic image is all about how Jim's body is prized and commodified; he's but one of

many muscular men whose bodies are glamorized by gay men, phy-
siques to be coveted in all senses of the word. Except, in this scenario,
Jim's body is to remain so untouchable that the (paid-for fantasy) allows only for respectful gazing, for a requisite distance between Jim
and the man who clearly clamors for Jim's body—and who takes a
particular kind of pleasure from having control over it, however fleeting and impersonal it may be. When you stop and think about it too
much, the scenario has a melancholic twinge to it. Butch-looking men
(in cowboy gear, but really in any kind of masculine drag) are forever
to be seen but not touched. Wanted but never reached, a dynamic
we're meant to replicate in fantasies that are in turn copies of fantasies
fed to us by magazines, by porn, by society at large.

The preamble to *La ley del deseo* ends in a similar mise-en-abyme
fashion. Before we get too comfortable (or, arguably, too hot and
bothered) by the images of the young man pleasuring himself under
order, Almodóvar cuts away from the erotic tableau and shows us a
pair of middle-aged men tasked with dubbing the scene at hand. They
dutifully run their lines (and moans) and, in so doing, yank us out
of the fantasy featuring the young stud. The scenario turns out to
be part of a project called *El paradigma del mejillón*, a film directed
by *La ley del deseo*'s main character, Pablo Quintero (Eusebio Poncela), that's being screened in the fictional world of Almodóvar's film.
Such a labyrinthine setup is characteristic of the Spanish filmmaker,
whose plots are spidery Russian nesting dolls that constantly twist and
turn into themselves. On that first viewing, once I managed to stop
blushing, I clicked *play* again and found myself enamored with the
obscenely complicated plot that followed.

All these decades later, I still recall how vividly that first scene
struck me dumb. It felt like my own shameful desires had been ex-
cavated and put on-screen for my own pleasure. Almodóvar had
conjured up an image that was for far too long the most erotic fantasy I could muster: a man in briefs, an image that captured the

confidence-exuding masculinity I envied and the soft vulnerability I craved. As I stood, every morning, in front of the full-length IKEA mirror I'd purchased for my dorm (the first time I'd ever had such a luxury in my own room), I wavered between wishing I'd be so admired as to be told to get on all fours and pleasure myself, and wanting to find someone who'd be so intoxicated by me that he'd do all I asked of him. This is why, perhaps, both Rechy and Almodóvar incorporate the mirror into their erotic scenarios: for many gay men like myself, the mirror was the first place where we could play out our own sexual fantasies. Yet that reflected image in front of me was also the source of many of my anxieties. On certain days, that reflection fueled (fuels, still) my most angst-ridden thoughts: I wasn't (am not) as muscular as I wish I were. I wasn't (am not) close to looking like the man I lust after. And if I couldn't be (am not) that, how could I find someone who'd lust after me? When I catch myself in the mirror, I'm always seeing double, watching myself through the eyes of others, at times with envy, sometimes with longing, almost always with a mix of both.

Doubles, of course, play a key role in *La ley del deseo*. Not for nothing did Almodóvar get Banderas to play a character named Antonio. And while that unnamed young man at the beginning first took my breath away, I could never have prepared myself for what Banderas later brings to the screen with the kind of white briefs that prologue scene so eroticizes. As the tortured young man who shares his first name, Banderas is a knot of contradictions. He's a predator who wishes to be preyed upon, a cocky young fanboy who wants to be wanted by Poncela's Pablo. When we watch Antonio leave the movie theater screening *El paradigma del mejillón* to jerk off in a restroom stall, it's clear he wishes to be the young man being ordered around by an imperious director. As he stalks Pablo later in the film, we see that there's a terrified and terrifying danger in Antonio's eyes. His desire to both be and be wanted by Pablo is too much; it eventually leads him to murder, his sadistic tendencies no match for the wanton tenderness he craves from his beloved.

If a plot description gifts him the label of a villain (he lies and connives and, yes, even kills), Almodóvar's final sequences make him also a tragic hero. Antonio is a young man who does not know how to elicit rather than demand desire. He's both too cunning and too romantic: when Pablo outright tells him he's not interested, Antonio badgers him and eventually coerces him into a well-worn version of domesticity: two men making a life together as lovestruck boyfriends. It's only later, when Antonio refuses to let Pablo go, that the filmmaker, still pining over the young boyfriend who'd recently left him, realizes he has no need for someone as green and clingy as Antonio. But Antonio doesn't take no for an answer. He makes himself indispensable to Pablo, helping him shower and doting on him every chance he gets, muscling his way into every nook and cranny of Pablo's life. As he finds himself more forcefully rejected, Antonio becomes a poster boy for toxic masculinity. Citing Leo Bersani's infamous "Is the Rectum a Grave?" essay, critic Paul Julian Smith (author of *Desire Unlimited: The Cinema of Pedro Almodóvar*) nails exactly why Antonio is such a complicated character, capturing the vexing relationship the Spanish filmmaker has with socially sanctioned ideals of manhood: "The peculiar paradox for gay men is that we both struggle against definitions of maleness which oppress us, and incorporate those definitions which we 'carry within us as permanently renewable sources of excitement.'" Antonio, he notes, is coded as "straight-acting": "he represents a certain intolerant and inflexible notion of masculinity . . . whose violation we can most enjoy and regret." He may stand in as an avatar for the kind of men who'd kill us, yet in doing so, he's also a distillation of a kind of man we're all socialized to want. To desire. Even to aspire to. And yes, as Smith notes, to violate.

Antonio is one of Banderas's greatest performances. There's something raw about it, as if Almodóvar had understood the lurking violence underneath the kind of magnetic charm Banderas so exudes. In fact, many of their collaborations mine that latent violence, lacing it with a pulsating eroticism. Almodóvar first encountered Banderas (born José Antonio Domínguez Bandera; it was Almodóvar's idea to add an extra *s* to his last name) in a theater production of *La hija del aire* where the filmmaker was captivated by the young actor's legs. Soon enough, he cast him in his second feature film, the 1982 sex romp/thriller comedy *Laberinto de pasiones*. Banderas played Sadec, an attractive young man we first meet when he's picked up by a foreign prince who's keeping his identity a secret in Madrid, and who later falls madly in love with Sexilia, a young woman who's curing her nymphomania with psychotherapy. Even amid such an outlandish plot, Antonio's charisma and sex appeal are undeniable—already he was driving both men and women wild. That Sadec was also a terrorist was a clear example of the way Almodóvar keyed into something else about Banderas's on-screen persona: there was always a hint of danger in him.

The filmmaker would better deploy this quality in their next two collaborations: in 1986's *Matador*, the then-twenty-six-year-old played Ángel, a tortured young man who decides to take responsibility for a string of murders likely committed by his bullfighting teacher; and then, of course, Antonio in *La ley del deseo*. And while Almodóvar gave him a reprieve with the straight-man (pun intended) role in his breakout comedy *Mujeres al borde de un ataque de nervios*, their next two films—shot more than two decades apart—again made Banderas exploit the darkened edges of his seductive appeal. In 1989's *¡Átame!* he played a mental patient who kidnaps a former porn actress in hopes of she'll fall in love with him, and in 2011's *La piel que habito* he played a plastic surgeon seeking revenge following the rape of his daughter. Sexual violence is at the heart of how Banderas's men interact with the female characters in both films, making Almodóvar's plots teeter close to unsavory territory when it comes to their decidedly thorny takes on female agency and desire. Which is what makes *La ley del deseo* all the more fascinating. Almodóvar weaponized Banderas's sex appeal—the very kind that would make him the face of the "Latin lover" in nineties Hollywood, equally able to get Madonna to swoon over him in front of his wife in *Truth or Dare* as to get Tom Hanks to praise his allure in an Oscar acceptance speech—in order to explore a young man's vexed relationship with his homosexuality. This Antonio character is basically a 1980s Spanish version of *The Talented Mr. Ripley*, another queer-themed thriller of sorts where doubles and same-sex desires collide and collude to tell a story about beautiful men and their dangerous insecurities. There is clearly something alluring and disturbing about men like Antonio, men who believe no one would turn them away. Men who know their bodies command everyone's attention and yet who wallow in the insecurity that desirability engenders.

Here's where Almodóvar clearly understood something about Banderas that Hollywood never has: Antonio was an entrancing character precisely because he was both the image of inviolate masculinity and the most fitting example of its fragility. By the time he crossed over (in 1992's *The Mambo Kings*, truly slipping into the "Latin lover" stereotype with the requisite flair), U.S. casting directors and filmmakers saw in Banderas's striking good looks and silky black hair merely a handsome, brooding foreigner who was best suited to blow stuff up (see *Desperado* and *Assassins*), woo pretty women (*Two Much*, *Original Sin*), and sometimes, even get to do both at the same time (*The Mask of Zorro*). There's always been an edge to Banderas's beauty, but Hollywood has rarely done more than blunt it. Almodóvar, instead, sought to unpack why men who looked like Antonio (character and actor alike) so beguiled us.

Not that I was unpacking the intricacies of Almodóvar's film that first time I watched it in the privacy of my dorm room. I was much too entranced by Banderas's spry body, which the Spanish director captures and displays for our lascivious enjoyment. Whenever he's naked, or merely wearing a pair of briefs, Antonio commands your attention. He's menacing even when he's being coy. An homme fatale who slowly makes *La ley del deseo* twist itself into a labyrinthian plot that gives Hitchcock a run for his money (it involves exchanged letters sent under pseudonyms, a murder atop a lighthouse, a trans woman's love affair with her father, a pair of estranged siblings, a stage production of Jean Cocteau's *La voix humaine*, and even a bout of amnesia), Antonio is constantly seducing the viewer. Often without much clothing to speak of. In the film's climax, which follows a kidnapping, a police standoff, a steamy love scene, and an impending suicide, he's wearing nothing more than, you guessed it, a pair of white briefs.

After kidnapping Pablo's sister Tina (Carmen Maura) and releasing her only once Pablo gives himself up, Antonio finds the world slowly encroaching on him. The private oasis he wishes he could construct with Pablo can no longer be. The police have finally caught up with him and it's only a matter of time until he's set to atone for the murder of Pablo's ex-boyfriend. Yet in the final moments Pablo and Antonio have together, Almodóvar stresses the true connection the two have forged. After sharing a passionate moment together in bed, followed by a tender kiss, Antonio rises, leaving his lover behind. By this point in the film he's stripped down to nothing, literally. He's as vulnerable as he's ever been, at last open to what Pablo's world could have offered him. Yet there's no way forward; it's why he grabs a gun and, before Pablo can do anything, shoots himself, collapsing on the floor. Even with a cast on his leg (don't ask), the filmmaker approaches his young lover and embraces him, grieving already for the life they could've had. In his extended study of the film, scholar José Quiroga pauses on this moment, noting how it is reminiscent of Michelangelo's *Pietà*. Yet such a reference can't quite capture what Almodóvar is getting at, for in holding Antonio in his arms, Pablo's pose "also evokes, more relevantly, an Achilles mourning the death of his lover Patroclus. As a reference," he adds, "it is a classic scene of homosexual love and bonding—two men who have been hurt by misfortune, war, and the struggle for existence—and it openly condenses the dramatic form that love takes at the moment of mourning." For Quiroga this is an "iconic homosexual image," one that ties into both Greco-Roman and Catholic aesthetics (they are, as it happens, standing right in front of a lit altar). But more importantly, it is the fact that they're all but naked (in briefs, Antonio's white, Pablo's baby blue). Just as Almodóvar had turned their intertwined naked bodies into an instantly recognizable portrait of same-sex intimacy after their first sexual encounter, here he stresses that tenderness again but ravages it with the spoils of violence.

Which brings us back to Calvin Klein, to the spirit of that 1982 ad that, like *La ley del deseo*, helped make the male body a gleaming object to be desired in public. But Hintnaus's original ad, in calling up the athletic body—he was an Olympian, after all—demanded we understand its standards as reaching back to a time when masculine beauty and masculine force couldn't be disentangled; not for nothing was it shot in Santorini, not too far from where Greco-Roman fighters like Achilles and Patroclus once roamed. For even in Hintnaus's languor there is the suggestion of power: his toned thighs and chest, bronzed by the sun, are a reminder of their ability. There's provocation even in his posed slumber. Writing about Weber's photographs of attractive young men at the turn of the century for *The New York Times* ("Beefcake for the Masses," the headline read), critic Herbert Muschamp distilled what made the photographer's work so intriguing—by quoting a psychoanalyst of all people. "Jacques Lacan said, 'Love is giving something you haven't got to someone who doesn't exist.' Ouch! But I would say the same thing about shopping. You can buy yourself a pair of Calvin Klein briefs, a Versace shirt or some cargo pants from Abercrombie & Fitch. But you can't give yourself the appearance of the models wearing these garments in Bruce Weber's photographs. In fact, not even Bruce Weber's models can give themselves this appearance." The reason? "These models do not exist."

They are but "figments of Weber's imagination," where they remain mere "passive objects."

This is why Antonio (and the fictional Antonio, I guess) is so unsettling. Though he may be a figment of Almodóvar's imagination, he manages to embody the passivity Weber captures in his photographs, but he's given an active role to play. He may begin as the young hustler in briefs letting himself be so wanted, but by the end of the film he's that Lacanian figure who's given love at the moment when he ceases to exist. Here we could further push back against Muschamp's musings on Weber's still-framed beefcakes: there is now an entire generation that has grown up with these images, freely available on billboards and ads and films and, most recently, on Instagram posts and Twitter alt pics, on TikTok videos and OnlyFans accounts. No longer are these men frozen statues coyly begging for our gaze. They're walking and talking (and cumming) real-life men who know just how to be wanted.

Far away from the mundanity of a department store, where the bounty of half-naked men often forced me to find distractions (a backpack held at an awkward angle, a sudden urge to go to the restroom) to hide my crotch in public lest an unintended hard-on give away the lustful thoughts they inspired, *La ley del deseo* animated those same erotic impulses. Almodóvar was the first director I saw turn his erotic gaze (that same one I deployed while shopping for underwear, the kind Weber captured in his CK photos) onto his male actors. It's what makes that first scene so powerful. To see a young man so casually flaunt his body and offer it up for the unseen director guiding his erotic fantasy is a perfect portrait of what made Almodóvar's films so eye-opening for a college kid awestruck by the sight of his own body in a pair of briefs in his full-length dorm mirror.

That reflection, which for so long had unnerved me in the way it aroused me, finally felt like a safe space. It witnessed my ever-growing fascination with my body as well as the many brands of briefs I soon began to accumulate. Colorful aussieBums that promised to enhance what I was packing. Suggestive Andrew Christians whose tight fit left little to the imagination. Athletic 2(X)IST pairs that conjured up locker-room fantasies. And yes, even a couple of classic Calvin Kleins for good measure. All helped me try to be as fearless and unguarded as that young man who goes from rubbing himself up against the mirror to an empty bed where he struggles but eventually utters the words he's clearly always wanted to say out loud: "Fóllame!"

8.

Balls Out

As magazine titles go, *SoHo*, short for "Sólo para Hombres" or "Just for Men," is as blunt as they come. First launched in 1999 in the hopes of giving Colombian men a publication all to themselves, this magazine was obviously modeled on the likes of *Esquire* and *GQ*, even as its covers were always closer to *Playboy* and *Maxim*. To celebrate its twentieth anniversary, here's how its editors summed up the magazine's budding history: "Women of unsettling beauty, seen through the best lenses, alongside stories full of wonder, humor, irony and extravagance." Such lofty ambitions are what had made *SoHo* one of the most widely read publications in Colombia at the turn of the century. With its audience neatly identified in its title and explicitly addressed in its pages, *SoHo* became a self-appointed bastion of contemporary Colombian masculinity. Its sex columns' headlines (everything from "The Best Positions" and "The 19 Things You Shouldn't Do" to "Three's Company") gave it the air of an urbane and cosmopolitan publication, keenly attuned to the modern man. Yet, as with Hugh Hefner's iconic mag, *SoHo* readers surely subscribed less for the investigative reporting or the satirical columns than for the chance to see local models and actresses baring it all in photo shoots that knowingly pushed the limits of what a "tasteful nude" could look like.

Over its first few monthly issues, *SoHo*'s covers seemed driven by increasingly raised bets: How suggestive a face can we get our models to make? How few items of clothing can we get them to wear? How much more can we accentuate their breasts? How much cleavage can we get away with? Nipples pierced through obscenely thin fabrics. Push-up bras more than lived up to their name. Carefully tousled sheets dutifully covered just what they needed to. Every cover image was designed to capture (and dream up) erotic scenarios its readers could and would giddily flesh out themselves. This was what men were called to do. To watch. To ogle. To lust after. All within the safe space of a magazine designed for them.

Such raised bets continued for months on end. So much so that, for its thirty-ninth issue, the magazine finally introduced its first topless cover model. In the pages of the magazine, model Juliana Galvis wrote about her motivation for taking part in the then-eyebrow-raising cover feature. She put it in simple terms that reflected *SoHo*'s raison d'être when it came to nudity: "Lo hice porque no quiero estar en un país en el que el escándalo todavía sea un cuerpo humano, un desnudo hecho con estética." She didn't want to live in a country that still gasps itself into a scandal at the sight of a human body. She wasn't posing naked. She was posing for a nude portrait. The distinction lay in the context; there was an artistry to her cover image. Nudity (not nakedness), both *SoHo* and Galvis insisted, was nothing to be scandalized about. The fact that *SoHo* only put its stock on female nudity wouldn't be a concern until 2007. For the September issue of that year, and the most talked-about cover yet, *SoHo* unveiled *SoHo para mujeres*. If you turned the magazine over, you were greeted with a second cover featuring a rarity: a male model. A fully nude one at that. Shipped with a fig leaf you could peel off, the cover left nothing to the imagination.

SoHo para mujeres, as cumbersome a title as you could ask for (spelled out, it was basically "just for men for women"), was conceived as a way to even the stakes. As its editors explained in a 2012 piece looking back over the first five years of this annual experiment, their move to carve a space for the female *SoHo* reader was in keeping with the groundbreaking work they saw themselves doing from the start. "¿Cómo editar una revista para satisfacer los intereses masculinos y evitar los desgarros machistas? ¿Cómo tomar fotos eróticas de mujeres, hacer de ellas un objeto de deseo, y a la vez no untarse del despreciable machismo que a lo largo de décadas ha consumido el mundo?" Namely, how do you edit a magazine that satisfies masculine interests and avoids their machista trappings? How can you shoot erotic images of women, make them objects of desire, and at the same time not smear yourself with the despicable machismo that throughout decades has consumed the world? The answers to these rhetorical questions, the piece implied, were to be found in *SoHo*. The publication saw itself as exemplifying a new kind of Colombian masculinity, one that necessarily left machismo behind. Their readers were interested in pleasing their women. They weren't afraid to admit they could be vain. They were eager to break taboos and to move forward in life as more open-minded versions of themselves. What better way to do this than to not only create an offshoot brand aimed exclusively at women but to launch it with the most provocative cover they'd ever shot?

The central theme for that inaugural issue was "women's vengeance": "las mujeres se vengaban de lo que los hombres hacemos en *SoHo* con ellas." Women would even the score for all that men did to them in the pages of *SoHo*, an admission that inadvertently revealed whose agency was always at stake in the magazine's pages. Here the battle of the sexes raged on. Compared with those explosive, come-hither photographs, though, this groundbreaking cover felt all the more demure. The black-and-white image of soccer player Faustino "Tino" Asprilla was very much the inverse of a regular *SoHo* cover in that it obviously bracketed sex out of the equation. Posed with two dark feathered wings behind him, one hand covering his chest, the other his abdomen (a bright-orange fig leaf keeping him modest, the better to display him on magazine racks all over the country), the Black soccer player evoked both religious iconography and classical aesthetics in one image. His brow slightly furrowed, he came across not as an object to be lusted after but one to be admired, like a marble statue. One that lacked erotic pull. *SoHo* only rarely offered up full-frontal female nudity (the vulva, it seems, occupies an even more taboo place in our visual economy than even a flaccid penis), but it was clear it could at first only let us admire the fully nude male body so long as sex was off the table.

Later *SoHo para mujeres* covers would, thankfully and cannily, more aggressively sexualize their subjects: actor Juan del Mar posed as a bullfighter, a red cape replacing the modesty fig leaf; photographer Raul Higuera posed shirtless staring straight at his camera, an erection clearly visible through his denim pants; porn actor Nacho Vidal flexed his rock-hard body as he held a sign over his crotch ("You really wanna see it? Find it on page 92," it read); actor Juan Pablo Raba, on his knees with his back (and ass to us), arms handcuffed behind him, stared at us in naked, coy defiance. Throughout all these images, and the attendant features and spreads that accompanied them, was a simple truth: the male body as an object of lust was a rare and rarified thing; the issue came out only once a year, after all.

If the female body has long been commodified to be gazed upon— dissected for clinical reasons and lusted after for erotic ones—the male body has remained, for much of Western culture's last two centuries, buttoned up, away from prying eyes. It's but one reason Ken looks neutered; Barbie may not boast any nipples or genitals either, but she at least gets to show off her buxom bosom. Granting itself claims to authority as well as universality, masculinity has rarely offered itself up for examination; it has always been subject, never object. Whether understood through Judeo-Christian ideas of shame and nakedness, or psychoanalytic ones of power and legibility courtesy of Freud and

Lacan, there's no escaping that the male body in general, and the penis in particular, has become as inviolate as it is invisible.

Both arrow and target, the penis does feel like it belongs hidden, tucked (not literally) away from our prying eyes. As a barometer of sexual urges, it is as blunt an erotic instrument as you're likely to find. Made visible, it cannot make its own interests unknown. From Saint Augustine (who'd been ruled by "the law of lust that is in my member") to Philip Roth's Portnoy ("When the prick stands up, the brains are as good as dead!"), the inconvenience of a boner that nevertheless rules over impulses suppressed cannot be denied. As Susan Bordo puts it in *The Male Body*, men are "not supposed to be slaves to sexual moods and needs, to physical and emotional dependency. They are supposed to think objectively—to think like Man with a capital letter, discerner of Eternal Truth, the Universal Subject of History, Philosophy, Religion. They're not supposed to think with their penises!" This explains why an out-of-sight, out-of-mind philosophy has guided pop culture's understanding of boner and penis alike. The way in which a man's lower body reveals such an unruly physicality has long been cast off from our visual economy, best kept zippered up. This has led to male nudity being conceived as incessantly eroticized on the one hand and as emasculating vulnerability on another. But perhaps more to the point, male nudity, as I came to understand it, could only ever be conceived as being offered up for women's pleasure—even, or especially, if such an imagined audience was dreamed up by men.

A whole ten years before Colombian readers of *SoHo* would be greeted with a black-and-white portrait of Asprilla, I was learning about the preciousness of everyday male nudity from the unlikeliest of sources: a sleeper hit of a British comedy.

The Full Monty does not and should not feel like an obvious companion piece to a glossy Colombian magazine designed for (let's face it, moneyed, privileged) men. Yet their incongruousness is the point. Miles away (and but two years before) *SoHo* was first published, Peter

Cattaneo's 1997 comedy about working-class men in the town of Sheffield coping with the steel industry's financial collapse served as a timely meditation on the anxieties of masculinity in a changing world. More than that, of course, this was a film obviously about something I was very interested in as a horny closeted teenager: male strippers. Sure, these weren't your average strippers. (I had to wait for Steven Soderbergh and Channing Tatum to give me a taste of that world in 2012's *Magic Mike*.) But at the edge of many of *The Full Monty*'s scenes lay the prospect—the possibility, in fact—of male nudity. It's teased for us at the beginning and hinted at with increasing fervor the closer we get to its climactic final number. The film operates like a proper strip show, luring us with the promise of skin, seductively teasing us with what's yet to come, giving us an ass cheek here and a thong-ful dance there, before, alas, refusing us the promise of its title, leaving us wanting more.

Writing about penis representation in 1990s American films, Peter Lehman notes, "it is no coincidence that the most traditional men have been comfortable with the silence surrounding the penis and its absence or careful regulation within representation." There's an element of shame here. Of undue importance being thrusted (no pun intended) onto the penis as symbol that leaves the penis as a limb out to dry. For Lehman, this invisibility contributed to a kind of "phallic mystique": "The penis is and will remain hidden until such time as we turn the critical spotlight on it."

The Full Monty feels like a perfect example of this mystique. The film, in fact, refuses to show us what its title advertises. For the penis is always what's promised, never what's delivered. Yet by its absence, it truly comes to dominate the plot. For years I felt cheated because of this. There were plenty of films I'd watch where I'd handily come across full-frontal female nudity. There I was catching the ridiculously bonkers *The Devil's Advocate* on cable television and a scene with a fully nude Charlize Theron would materialize. Here I was dreamily staring into Leonardo DiCaprio's eyes aboard the Titanic from the comfort of a packed movie theater only to find myself blushing at the sight of Kate Winslet in the buff.

My curiosity about seeing dicks on-screen was, let's be blunt, more hormonal than anything else. We didn't have locker rooms and showers at school. And before I perfected the emergency close-out-your-browser-and-wipe-your-browsing-history maneuver while surfing the net on my mom's office computer (using dial-up, no less), I didn't really have much to go on when it came to male anatomy. What I knew was that the female body, whether it was being paraded in swimsuits in the Miss Colombia pageant or eroticized in those softcore French porn features I stumbled onto on late-night cable, was always up for consumption. To be ogled at. To be lusted after. Men watched; women were watched. Simple as that.

You'd think this is what would've drawn me to *The Full Monty* (whose Spanish-language title was a lot more explicit than its hazy British slang one: "Todo o nada," all or nothing). Except it was my mom who was initially enamored with the hilarious premise behind the film. I can't recall how or why or when we first watched it together as a family. But it became one we revisited often following the year it charmed its way to the Oscars. The little comedy that could went head-to-head with that DiCaprio/Winslet behemoth of a blockbuster, a touching Helen Hunt/Jack Nicholson rom-com, an icy LA-set neo-noir that netted Kim Basinger a win, and an unlikely Ben Affleck/Matt Damon writing vehicle that gave funnyman Robin Williams his golden statue. Which is to say, even as a fourteen-year-old, I was aware that the love we harbored for this small comedy was shared by audiences all over the world. It's one of the reasons it's stayed with me even as it has been, maybe unfairly, eclipsed in the two decades since it premiered. (Quirky small-town-set British comedies, after all, have become a genre unto their own.) Or, perhaps, it's the fact that I saw it with my mom, that I got to watch a film that grappled with sophisticated ideas about how manliness was changing in the comfort of our home without the requisite snickers or blushes that would otherwise have greeted talk of male strippers. A film like *Election*, which we watched the following year, remains one of the most uncomfortable viewing experiences I've ever had: we thought we were signing up for a funny high school flick, but its themes of sexual assault, power dynamics, and yes, even an in-your-face lesbian subplot were too much for us. Alexander Payne's slippery black comedy was almost immediately banished from our consciousness; best not let its deliciously rotten humor fester in our home. In contrast, a feel-good comedy like *The Full Monty* was a perfect four-quadrant project. It cuts through its themes (which include, in case you've forgotten, unemployment, grief, divorce, parenting, body image, and yes, homosexuality) with such palatable humor that it feels tailor-made for a wide-eyed reassessment. Not to see whether it "holds up" or whether we can judge it by contemporary standards, but to see what it can teach us about mainstream conversations around masculinity and the nude male body.

It's easy to know where to begin: in the world of *The Full Monty*, a man undressed was shamefully emasculating at worst and uproariously funny at best. This is the note on which the film begins. When Gaz (Robert Carlyle) and his buddy Dave (Mark Addy) come across an ad for the male strippers that are coming into town, his first instinct is to dismiss them. He resorts, of course, to homophobic and emasculating language: "you know where to find me when you're tired of them poofs," he pelts at the women lining up for the show before continuing his (otherwise unprompted) tirade. "I mean, look at the state of that," he says while pointing at the impressive physique featured in said poster: "I don't know what you've got to smile about. I mean, he's got no willy for starters, has he? There's nowt in the gym that'll help you there, mate."

Willy-less poofs. That's what these men are to Gaz. He can't fathom the vanity necessary to spend hours at the gym to look like an

Adonis without wanting to use those muscles as stand-ins for below-the-belt insecurities, nor the confidence needed to strut your stuff and let yourself be admired by a throng of women without demeaning that very choice. These anxieties, about what it means to be a man ("You call them Chippendales men?" he scoffs later), are what drive this otherwise affable British comedy. As Roger Ebert succinctly put it in his three-star review, "*The Full Monty* is about more than inventiveness in the face of unemployment. It's about ordinary blokes insisting that their women regard them as men—job or no job." Ever the wordsmith, Ebert's choice of *regard* is, as the film stresses, very much the point. The men in Sheffield are paralyzed by how their wives (and ex-wives) see them. They worry, in fact, that they may not be seen or needed for much longer.

When Gaz and Dave sneak into the venue where the Chippendales are performing, it's the sight of women owning their desires so openly that shatters their confidence. Women, as they secretly witness when they hear a woman peeing standing up, are taking over things that have long felt exclusive to them. Staging that scene in a men's restroom, as literal a safe space for men as screenwriter Simon Beaufoy could've envisioned, further highlighted the sense that the Sheffield guys, who spend much of their days in a dull job center where no jobs seem to ever materialize, see their world shrinking. They are no longer masters of their domains—not at home and not in these kinds of public spaces. It is their women who have become the breadwinners in their families and who can afford a night out to see some men dance for their pleasure. In keeping us focused on Gaz and Dave, Catteneo doesn't show us much of what the Chippendales men are selling; instead, what we see are the frenzied faces of women who, perhaps for the first time in their lives, get permission to hoot and holler after willing, limber men. It's no surprise that, for Gaz and Dave, the world suddenly feels topsy-turvy.

Three years after the film became a worldwide hit, a musical adaptation landed on Broadway. Nimbly relocating the premise from Sheffield in the United Kingdom to Buffalo, New York, playwright Terrence McNally (*Kiss of the Spider Woman, Love! Valour! Compassion!*) and composer David Yazbek (*Dirty Rotten Scoundrels*) keyed into these fears in the two numbers that set the plot in motion, the aptly titled "It's a Woman's World" and its follow-up, "Man." The former, sung by the women enjoying the Chippendales performers, establishes how little agency the unemployed men in their town have: "Who's got power? Who's got juice? Who's got the money?" the song begins, asking rhetorical questions that are answered by the song's very title: "It's a woman's world." It may be just one night, but Georgie (Dave's wife) and her friends are more than happy to be (or merely feel) on top for once. It's no wonder an entrepreneurial guy would see in his strip-and-get-rich idea a way to pay the alimony he's been neglecting, as well as a way to reclaim his role as a man.

That's exactly what fuels his number, "Man." This is the moment when Jerry (Gaz, given here a more palatable name) eggs on his friend to take control of his life again, to embrace the man he is, and to find in that strength the confidence to bare it all. The lyrics are so outsized that they call up a caricature of its titular figure. His hands are rough and his back is hairy. His talk is tough and his smell is scary—and, lest you'd even think of it, he's no fairy. He loves to carve the beef. He hates Tom Cruise but listens to Lee Marvin. He's a "boot-wearin', beer-drinking, Chevy-driving man." Part of Jerry/Gaz and Dave's arc necessarily has them move away from such a rigid idea of what a man can be; by the end, they're holding a thong in front of a throng of women.

In the original Broadway run, Jerry was played by Patrick Wilson. Yes, the Patrick Wilson who would shortly thereafter play, in quick succession, a closeted Mormon who publicly strips to try to win over a man in HBO's *Angels in America*, a totally fuckable "prom king" who knows his way around a lurid laundry room in Todd Field's infidelity drama *Little Children*, an idealized high school jock who continues to live rent-free in his old girlfriend's mind in Jason Reitman and Diablo Cody's raucous ode to disgruntled adulthood in *Young Adult*, and a hazy, possibly dreamed-up dreamboat of a Brooklyn fling in one of the most-discussed bottle episodes of *Girls*'s run. Which is all to say, compared to Carlyle's Gaz, Wilson's Jerry was less a picture of a wiry-looking, ordinary British bloke than a portrait of an all-American guy on the outs, though one who could elicit his fair share of exhilarated yelps from the audience before he even suggests taking his clothes off.

Strippers invite our gaze. They clamor for it. Given that stripping requires a spectator, a relationship, in fact, between gazer and gazed that is fluid and dynamic, it's hard to draw any clear-cut categories about the agency of those involved—more so when we talk about male strippers. For, in inviting our lustful gazes, male strippers seemingly break away from the so-called natural order of things wherein men watch and women are watched (how quaint). Yet, no matter what Gaz/Jerry may say, stripping is no emasculating activity. Or rather, it is so enmeshed with rigid ideas about masculinity that it's hard to disentangle it so easily and say that a man dropping down to a thong and shaking his ass for dollar bills is merely inverting the sexual politics at work.

Here's where that *other* famous film about male strippers better illuminates these issues. *Magic Mike*, more so than *The Full Monty*, relished depicting the act of stripping. For Cattaneo the dancing and stripping Gaz and his friends do is a series of punchlines: you see Gaz stumbling while taking his shirt off because he refuses to dispense with his cigarette; you find that the only way these working men know how to learn any kind of choreography is through celebratory soccer moves. This is why the film's final image, with the spotlight blinding us and denying us what its title promises, feels so appropriate. It's a sleight of hand that keeps the specifics of their performance out of our minds. Not so in *Magic Mike*. From the moment Matthew McConaughey's Dallas first invites us into the world of the Xquisite Strip Club, Steven Soderbergh's camera lovingly replicates the hungry looks this leather cowboy emcee elicited onstage. There's a sensuality that pervades a lot of the film. It's not just that McConaughey and (former exotic dancer turned actor) Channing Tatum scorch up the screen with their sexy charisma (as do the rest of the self-proclaimed "Cock-Rocking Kings of Tampa"). It's that, unlike the comedic trappings of *The Full Monty*, *Magic Mike* knows that to properly immerse us in the world of its titular character means embracing the steamy sensory experience of being seated at a club and being encouraged to look.

When I caught *Magic Mike* (on opening weekend, no less) at a Manhattan theater with a group of gay male friends, I wasn't ready for the kind of screening I'd gotten us into. Surrounded by a group of rowdy, and rather drunk, filmgoers (mostly women, though with its fair share of groups like ours), the film at times became not about strippers but a strip show in itself. Perhaps this had to do with the film's aggressive marketing push, which all but promised a recorded Chippendales performance. That Soderbergh and screenwriter Reid Carolin had crafted an empathetic portrait of a wayward young man finding mentorship in a budding entrepreneur who weathered the 2009 financial collapse through stripping meant little to the audience around me, who seemed to clock out during much of the film's yellow-tinged scenes outside of Xquisite. They only came alive when Tatum or Alex Pettyfer or any of the other members of the film's ensemble strutted their stuff to songs like "It's Raining Men" and "Save a Horse (Ride a Cowboy)."

The excitement of such a scene, whether as captured by Cattaneo and Soderbergh, or witnessed in real life at an actual strip show, comes from the anticipation of nudity, its promise as much as its arrival. Thus, while nudity is the dreamed-up goal of a strip show, such titillation can only come from the body's relationship with what it's wearing, what it's taking off. A stripper costume isn't merely something to be dispensed with. It invokes characters and archetypes that enrich the performance. It's why the men at Xquisite all have specific looks they flaunt onstage. Like the figures Jerry sings about in "Man," the *Magic Mike* boys know the power there is in conjuring up familiar tropes before (quite literally) peeling back their layers: Matt Bomer turns a rigid preppy Ken doll into a sinuous thong-flaunting dancer; Joe Manganiello's Big Dick Richie handily makes his fireman routine a fiery affair; while Adam Rodriguez's Tito makes the most out of a navy uniform. When Mike takes "The Kid" (Pettyfer) clothes shopping, he makes clear that such choices are as central to the act as the dances and the moves (and the ass cheeks). More tellingly, it's obvious these costumes key into the fantasies these dancers are meant to inspire onstage; these imposing images of manhood (be they authority figures in uniform or neutered dolls meant to be ideal partners) get deployed by exotic dancers in order to break them apart. They encourage our wandering eyes to linger and maybe, just maybe, to dispel the images' everyday power in our own eyes.

Whose eyes, though? Women's, as it turns out.

McConaughey's Dallas puts it bluntly: "You see, baby, you're not just stripping. You are fulfilling every woman's wildest fantasies. All right? You are the husband that they never had. You are that dreamboat guy that never came along." That's the pep talk he gives The Kid: "You are the liberation!" he bellows as he instructs the young man on how to *not* take his clothes off like a twelve-year-old in a locker room. To do so, instead, like a man: "Who's got the cock?" he bellows, "You do!" The scene, set at a gym where the rest of the dancers are pumping their muscles and practicing their moves in front of the many mirrors that surround them, is aggressively heterosexual. Yet also distinctly homoerotic. McConaughey is wearing the tightest bike shorts you can imagine and a sleeveless crop top: his body is gleaming with sweat and his eyes glint with excitement, especially when he sidles up behind the shirtless Pettyfer and grinds up on him so as to better show him how to writhe. "Ain't time for a fucking fag joke," Dallas snaps at the bemused and perhaps a tad intimidated Kid, whose face does, for a second, capture the "No homo!" reaction Dallas no doubt anticipated. But the line also feels directed at the audience; a sweaty McConaughey is staring at the mirror where it feels like he's addressing us as much as The Kid. Whatever homoeroticism is inherent in this image is neutered with that one line, a reminder that this kind of stripping is about being a man, yes, but a man who's intent on pleasing women. Those of us who take pleasure in the skin-tastic stripping numbers Soderbergh lovingly shoots—as well as in a moment like this where tenderness and eroticism, camaraderie and mentorship commingle into something that looks like same-sex desire—have long needed to disentangle them from the very frames that surround them. We have had to look past the straightness Dallas insists on, the one he knows he's skirting away from when he gets up close and personal with The Kid. The move is both expansive (imagining a welcome intimacy between men) and restricting (only between certain kinds of men and with only women as imagined onlookers).

Compared to this, *The Full Monty*'s gay subplot involving two of Gaz's makeshift dancers falling for one another and eventually holding hands in public ("there's nowt as queer as folk," Gaz quips) seems not only quaint but quietly radical in comparison. True, the film never quite lingers on their budding relationship nor ever fleshes out how the rest of the boys feel about it or how the experience of dropping trou among a supportive group of men opened them up to the possibility of being together (where's *that* movie?). But the fact that there was a push for inclusion in the vision of unguarded (and disrobed) masculinity that closes out the film remains admirable in its own right.

Not so in *SoHo*, which peddled (unintentionally, perhaps) a kind of homophobia that remains all too familiar all these years later. Deviance from sexual norms was allowed—or acknowledged, I guess—but it was rarely embraced to the point where the hombres the magazine addressed felt included in such a formulation. This was clearest in the essays that dealt more openly with LGBTQ issues. Published as part of the men-geared articles in that *SoHo para mujeres* issue, as part of a series of "What it's like to have sex with . . ." articles ("a sexologist," "my professor," "a twin"—even "an oriental," yes, really), one article concerned itself with what it was like for a man to have sex with another man. Echoing that *Men Are from Mars* rhetoric again, the writer tried to make the point that, in his own experience, having sex with men opened him up to realizing he enjoyed being an animal in bed. Except, he didn't like to be either predator or prey (presumably his only choices because power imbalances are the only way he could understand sex). During his bisexual phase (his words) when he slept with both men and women, he came to realize that he'd rather be mauled by a lion than scratched by a pussycat (also his words): "Most women like to be cared for and loved only in certain ways. Men, we like to be swallowed whole however and wherever, to lose our modesty and play with whatever holes are so offered to us." Men are aggressive, women are passive. Men are driven by lust, women by emotion. The schematics in this testimonial are unsurprisingly dispiriting, especially in the way they imagine gay masculinity as merely replicating heterosexual masculinity . . . but with a lust for men. Aggression and violence are framed as inherent aspects of men, no matter who we're fucking. There's no room for softness; we're all lustful lions here eager to maul and be mauled by one another.

To read the rest of the issue was to get the sense that gay men were unwelcome interlopers—both in the pages that upheld a modern Colombian masculinity and in those that catered exclusively to women. Ever the footnotes or the unexplored subplots (as in *The Full Monty*), gay men were nothing more than cracks in the gendered cosmology being dreamed up. Best they be neutered on sight. That this was all tied up with issues of nudity—of who got to be lusted after and whose agency was at play in any one of those given interactions—is not surprising. For the naked male body has long been the repository for anxieties about what men should and could be.

This is what made an article that chronicled the seeming lack of male nudity in art history in *SoHo para mujeres* all the more enraging. As journalist Marianne Ponsford rightly points out, the male nude is curiously absent from our aesthetic vocabulary. Or rather, its appearances are always curiously circumscribed: images of a tortured Saint Sebastian and of a crucified Jesus are, after all, ubiquitous in museums and churches alike. Yet those naked male bodies are bodies in suffering; there's no eroticism to them. Or so she writes. Ponsford clearly wasn't familiar with the relentless way in which Saint Sebastian, for instance, has long been a queer figure whose suffering is eroticized, an example of the commingling of pain and pleasure that serves as an avatar for S&M sensibilities, and who, in the hands of Derek Jarman (the filmmaker behind 1976's *Sebastiane*) became a modern queer icon in his own right.

Then again, Ponsford spends much of her column bemoaning the fact that gay men first ushered the male nude into the mainstream. When she cites Robert Mapplethorpe, she adds that it's a pity (unfortunate, really) he was gay. Here again was another instance where it was men who were gazing. Women were left to blindly stumble through the world of artistic nudity. At the end of her diatribe she finds some hope: by the time of her writing she could point to ads by Lacoste Homme (for the "Style by Skin" campaign for its new toiletries line) and YSL (for its M7 fragrance), both of which turned naked men into sexual objects to be gazed at by women. "Esa es la gran revolución en la historia del desnudo masculino: la mirada que inmortaliza el cuerpo desnudo del hombre es, por fin, la mirada de una mujer," she writes; finally, women were allowed to ogle, their gaze was being immortalized. She missed, it seems, how the Lacoste TV ad wherein a naked man hops out of bed and lounges around his apartment wearing nothing but said branded fragrance (we only ever see him from behind or tastefully seated) was shot by renowned (and out gay) photographer Herb Ritts, while the YSL ad that so scandalized readers featuring martial arts star Samuel de Cubber sitting with his legs apart and his flaccid penis unobtrusively visible was conceived by Tom Ford (yes, another out gay figure).

If nothing else, such facts make Ponsford's complaint all the more urgent: the female gaze is still rather absent from our visual economy. But there's no denying her point still stands: these ads and images, homoerotically tinged as you or I may find them, were constructed with an imagined female audience in mind. At least the Lacoste one was. That commercial begs to be understood as an ad for a handsome boyfriend every girl would kill to have at home. Ford's boundary-pushing ad, on the other hand, was in line with the many controversial campaigns Ford had overseen at Gucci (including a 1997 one shot by Mario Testino featuring a nude Renaud Tison and a pair of briefs, and a suggestive 2001 photo by Terry Richardson where model JR Gallison held his belt like he would his own boner) and would later produce at Tom Ford, constantly pushing the limits of how male and female nudity could be deployed in fashion advertising campaigns. Collectively, these images suggest new ways of looking at nude and partly nude bodies.

When Dallas encourages The Kid in *Magic Mike* to connect with the women who are staring at him while he's stripping, he stresses the need to imagine himself being inside all of them—and to wait for that moment (he'll know the one) when he can "stick it." Metaphorically, of course. There is, both at the level of dialogue and in the film's visual vocabulary (one can't not focus on Pettyfer's defined abs as he squats and gyrates for McConaughey's benefit) an emphasis on hardness, on straining (it helps that the rest of the Xquisite crowd is quite literally

weight lifting right off frame). In what may be one of the most casually revealing lines from the film about how men approach their own
desirability, Dallas ends his makeshift training by urging Pettyfer's
character to "fuck that mirror like you mean it." He may be egged
on to make eye contact with the women he'll strip for, but ultimately,
such a performance demands he remain in control; there's a sense of
dominance Dallas wants The Kid to master.

In writing about male pinups, critic Richard Dyer isolates this dynamic. Even when they stare at you, the male pinup, he writes, seems
to stare right back at us, "as if he wants to reach beyond and through
and establish himself." Even (or especially) when naked, there's a degree of reticence, of restraint at work, a sense that to fully reveal oneself as a man remains an all-too-high cost to pay to let oneself be seen.
This is how the male body most willingly proffers itself to us in our
contemporary visual economy: seemingly hardened for our pleasure
yet knowingly denied for us in the flesh.

9.

Into the Future

FUTURITY IS A PRIVILEGE. THE ABILITY TO PROJECT YOUR-self into an unknown and uncertain future requires, after all, a lived-in groundedness in your here and now as well as a solid belief about the state of the then and there. To dream up a future for oneself is to leave the concept of precarity behind and embrace instead the promise of possibility.

Thinking ahead has never come easily to me. I am one of those people who bristles at those questions about where I see myself in five, ten, twenty years. This need to flesh out imaginary futures offers, I know, a solace for some; the idea presents folks with the comfort of a template. Yet these questions terrify me. They feel like traps. Not in that Greek tragedy sort of way where speaking something aloud will inevitably bring about an ironic demise. But in the sense that they beg me to instantiate myself in time; a future snapshot can only proceed from a present still frame. I run away from such future projections because I worry they'll freeze my current sense of self in place.

There are, to be fair, less metaphysical reasons why the future has long loomed as a temporal haze. As a teenager, for instance, the plans and paths laid out for me—by school, family, and society at large— were claustrophobic. I didn't want to go to university with the same people I'd gone to school with since I was five years old. I didn't want to find an office job once I graduated, nor a wife with whom I'd have the requisite amount of kids for my extended family to fawn over. The future never felt expansive growing up. It always closed up on and around me, throttling any other possibilities. Even when I tried to wrestle my self-image away from that nine-to-five family man, the alternative felt all the more fatalistic. What kind of future could a queer teen choose to build for himself when the threat of a virus inextricably linked with his sexual proclivities all but extinguished hope for any future at all? Stuck between what felt like opposing but equally damaging visions of myself, I did the only thing I could think of: I fled.

Well, not quite. I absconded abroad; forsaking any backup plans (I never applied to any Colombian universities, nor to any other university anywhere else), I bet on myself in the way only a naively ambitious eighteen-year-old can. The University of British Columbia was the only college in North America I could find that disbursed financial aid to international students—a full ride, no less. That's how I landed on arguably the most pretentiously titled scholarship imaginable: the Leader of Tomorrow Award. With no need to saddle my single working mom with tuition nor, as it happens, room and board expenses (I even got enough money to cover my books every semester), I spent the last few months of high school finally imagining a future away from Bogotá. But I never did color in that image. I only gave myself a horizon: Vancouver, which I'd been told was lovely and, weather-wise, akin to the temperate Andean feel of the city I was leaving behind. But that's where the vision stopped. Suddenly, untethered from the futures that had once been mapped out for me, I took it upon myself to let them go. For, as soon as I landed in Vancouver on a four-year student visa, and later in New Brunswick, New Jersey, in a similarly restrictive visa situation for what turned out to be an eight-year stint in grad school, the mere concept of a future was so enmeshed with immigration bureaucracy that it never felt worthy of contemplation.

Semester to semester, year to year, visa renewal to visa renewal. That's how I lived, my capacity to think beyond these calendrical bureaucratic units of time eventually stunted to the point that, when I got married and such strictures were finally lifted, I was left adrift, realizing I'd been forcing myself to live in the present with an unwavering (and yes, almost crippling) aggressive indifference to the future.

It didn't help that the one queer theory book I ended up gravitating toward as an undergraduate, and which became a totemic intellectual beacon throughout my (not-so-short-lived) academic career, was literally titled *No Future*. Lee Edelman's meditations on futurity helped reframe my worldview; with endlessly cascading sentences that relished a good play on words while looking at everything from Charles Dickens's novels to Alfred Hitchcock's films, the literary scholar armed me with enough ammunition to explain why, maybe at a core level, I never did give a damn about the future, mine or anyone else's. The future, as he explains, is kid's stuff. Literally. In Edelman's polemic, the structuring principle of politics is the figure of the Child; everything is done in their (arguably *his*) name. And so, wanting to push back against the notion of "reproductive futurism," which not only ignores but explicitly antagonizes anyone who's not committed to children in ways both figural and literal, Edelman arrives at his premise: queerness names the side of those *not* fighting for the children. Where pop culture, for instance, would have us root for Harry instead of Voldemort, cheer on Peter instead of Captain Hook, and forever be entranced by the promise of a "Tomorrow" that little orphan Annie sings about, Edelman proposes nixing the very futurity the figure of the Child stands for. "And so," he writes, "what is queerest about us, queerest within us, and queerest despite us is this willingness to insist intransitively—to insist that the future stop here."

Wasn't the future merely a recycled present, forever churning away the status quo in slightly tweaked iterations? While reading *No Future*, I kept thinking of the show *The Jetsons*, arguably one of the most dispiriting images of the future I've ever come across. Sure, there are bleaker provocations and propositions of what futures, dystopian and utopian alike, can look like. But within the sunny sitcom trappings of *The Jetsons* was precisely what Edelman conceptualized. Just as *The Flintstones* merely replicated the contemporary family sitcom in a fanciful version of the Stone Age, this Hanna-Barbera series imagined a world in 2062 where families had robot maids and all sorts of homemaker gadgets, yet their lives were not unlike those of anyone living in 1962, the year when the first episode aired on ABC. Here was a future that was a mere facsimile of the present; a hundred years into the future and George Jetson is still grinding away to provide for a wife who, in the opening sequence of the show, takes his entire wallet so she can enjoy a good time at the sky-high shopping center. Honestly, who would want that future?

Edelman's apathetic theory, which almost begs to be pilloried and parodied, both for its jargon-riddled sentences and its intentionally convoluted psychoanalytic readings, was a particularly welcome fit for an aggrieved young man itching to explain away his own reticence toward what he thought the world expected of him. Edelman reshaped my hopelessness into what felt then like a radical politics. But in doing so, he also calcified my own sense of time. I had no time for the future.

Except, of course, when it came to the movies. Well, one movie in particular.

I was twelve—thirteen at most—when I watched *The Fifth Element* for the first time. My brother, my sister, and I nestled around our mother in her king-sized bed, as we always did when we made time to watch a movie together at home. We were never the kind of family unit to make a big deal out of dinners together; we usually took our plates to our respective TVs. That meant our weekend movie viewings were as close as we got to quality family time. Sometimes this meant going to the malls in Bogotá to catch the latest family-friendly release at a Sunday matinee. That's where I first swooned over *Hercules*, a story about a scrawny boy who ends up finding his purpose once he hits the gym, and where we all first bawled our way through *Lilo & Stitch*, a story about a broken family that cut a little too close to home. Oftentimes it amounted to watching whatever was playing on cable. For a couple of months in 1998, a broken pay-per-view satellite channel meant we could catch *Contact* and *My Best Friend's Wedding* on loop as many times as we wanted, which I did, dutifully making Jodie and Julia twinned role models of my youth. And sometimes it involved a recent Blockbuster rental, which was always a mixed bag of compromises. Except for that time we got *Face/Off*, still an all-time family favorite. Turns out all we needed was an implausible but highly entertaining action film about a cop and a criminal swapping faces (yes, really) that stars two of Hollywood's most bonkers actors doing the most ridiculously uncanny impressions of one another.

On occasion, when our household veered away from family fare, we were guided by my mother's tastes. Her predilection was for films that fulfilled two simple requests: they needed to have a ruggedly handsome male lead, and they were required to feature an improbable plot centered, if not entirely dependent, on stuff blowing up. This was the reason *Face/Off* shot itself up to the top of our must-see pile; as a fervent *Saturday Night Fever* (and, more recently, *Look Who's Talking*) fan, my mom's affinity for John Travolta knew no bounds.

It's hard not to try to theorize why these actioners so speak to my mom. At a base level I know this preference is rooted in her unwavering belief in the escapist potential of pop culture. The reason she reads John Forsythe paperback novels, binges shows like *Star Trek*, and watches James Bond flicks with such fervor is because she's uninterested in finding her own world reflected back at her. Real life, she'll tell me time and time again, is messy and exhausting enough as it is; why would you want to encounter it in times of leisure when what you most want is to unplug, to disengage? For that's what she did on Friday nights when she went out with her boyfriend to watch the latest Arnold Schwarzenegger or Bruce Willis release. There was a welcome comfort in the worlds depicted there: you knew who the good guys were and who the bad guys were, and the plot unfolds efficiently enough to reward the former and punish the latter. Any film that deviated from well-worn formulas got not so much groans as endless diatribes from them both. In an anecdote my mom has not yet tired of repeating whenever we cite films she cannot stand, she calls up the night when, perhaps guided solely by the marquee appeal of one Nicolas Cage, she had to suffer through Spike Jonze's film *Adaptation*, whose title in Colombia sounded less obtuse (or meta): *El ladrón de orquídeas*. Literally borrowing the title from the nonfiction book screenwriter Charlie Kaufman was tasked with adapting—and which he instead remixed and retooled into a deranged satire about the film industry's obsession with gun-toting, drug-fueled, car-exploding Hollywood nonsense—the marketing suggested the film might have been one my mom could enjoy. It's about an orchid thief, after all. Yet, to judge by the way merely mentioning the film two decades later still riles her up, *Adaptation* remains one of the most reviled films she's ever had to sit through. It also happens to be one of my favorite movies of all time and the second 2002 Meryl Streep film a family member eviscerated in front of me at the time without knowing how much both films would come to mean to me in the years since (*The Hours*, to hear my grandmother tell it, was a morally repugnant story; she wished she could've sat through *Analyze This* a second time instead).

As a film, and as a conceit, really, *Adaptation* is about the lack of a narrative. About the anxiety over the lack of a narrative. In the fiction of the movie, Charlie (a balding Nicolas Cage) fears he's gotten in way over his head. How is he supposed to adapt a book about orchids written by Susan Orlean, whose meandering *New Yorker* prose values vibes over plot and scenes over story? He knows producers and audiences alike would be more titillated if he could somehow make this a drug-trafficking story. With some illicit romance thrown in for good measure. The kind of schlocky script his twin brother, Donald (also a balding Nicolas Cage) is intent on writing. But couldn't the thrill be found instead in Orlean's wistful words? In the beauty of the orchid? In a story that would not be propelled toward a known future, toward a familiar ending?

Needless to say that while my mom found the entire metafictional affair an insufferable mess, Kaufman, writer and character alike, is very much my shit. As *Eternal Sunshine of the Spotless Mind* and even more outré provocations like *Synecdoche, New York* and *I'm Thinking of Ending Things* attest, Kaufman is an artist obsessed with the concept of endings. Or rather, with non-endings. With the precarity of finality. His narratives constantly teeter away from any neat conclusions and push us instead to live in the anxiety the impetus toward ending things (be they a screenplay, a relationship, or a theater production) can generate. Haunted by the blank page—arguably a fear I've encountered more times than I'd like to count in finishing just this chapter alone—*Adaptation*'s Charlie resorts to genre conventions, to tried-and-true formulas, the very kind my mom so enjoys. The final act of that film hits every lazy action trope you can think of, all while making fun of them. Yet—and here's why *Adaptation* soars above its dour if tongue-in-cheek conceit—there's a sincerity on display here so that when Charlie is saved by his twin brother, Donald, who then dies in his arms, the cliché-riddled moment ends up feeling like a gut punch. Part of it has to do with Nicolas Cage's performance. Both of them, since he plays twins. But also the many Cage performances we'd all seen before.

Cage, who'd won an Oscar in 1995 for playing an alcoholic in *Leaving Las Vegas*, boasted—even by the time he shot *Adaptation*, though arguably this is even truer now as *The Unbearable Weight of Massive Talent* most recently proved—one of the most eclectic careers in Hollywood. A bona fide leading man who could anchor a maudlin ghost story of a romance in *City of Angels* as well as a preposterous action thriller in *Con Air*, Cage possesses a fearless brio on- and off-screen that make his take on Charlie and Donald Kaufman all the more intriguing. For if you were to sum up a quintessential Cage performance (a futile endeavor, for sure), you'd likely land on a variation of the word *intensity*. The best Cage performances (and here I should point out I'd easily place *Face/Off* right at the top) are master classes in controlled chaos. To watch Cage not just lose himself in a role but harness it around his own unhinged energy is always an electric experience. So to watch him cower into the shoes of an angst-ridden, self-deprecating screenwriter who constantly feels like he's taking up too much space when he's elbowing himself out of everyone's way, was a treat. As was watching him play Donald, whose unfalteringly sunny disposition borders on ignorance and serves as a twinned foil to his brother. In the final scene, as Charlie has finally figured out a way to end the screenplay he's unwittingly inserted himself into, and wonders (in voice-over, a screenwriting 101 no-no, he knows) who will play him in the film, we all get a laugh in at his one suggestion: Gerard Depardieu. There's something quite revelatory about seeing Cage land this line, a sense that even in Kaufman's wildest dreams he'd never have dared to imagine an actor like Cage to begin with. Yet therein lies the thrill at the end of *Adaptation*. Charlie ends up becoming the action hero he never knew he could be. Who better to play him, then, than *Face/Off*'s Nicolas Cage himself?

My mom's antipathy toward *Adaptation* likely also hinged on this brazen bait and switch. Where Kaufman, and myself, struggle with endings, my mom is unwavering in her belief in tidy, happy ones. She's the kind of reader who'll turn to the final pages of a novel to make sure she knows where she's headed and is assured that the destination is one she's comfortable arriving at. Where as a collective we're obsessed with avoiding spoilers, some of us steering clear of social media after our favorite RuPaul-hosted television series airs lest we learn who's sashayed away before we've been able to watch the lip sync that sent said queen home, my mom is all too happy to read up on plot twists and summaries for films and television shows she's set on watching. Her disregard for such preciousness about endings is such that, when she came back from watching *The Sixth Sense* on opening weekend, she talked at length about (spoiler alert) Bruce Willis having been a ghost the entire time, an unwanted revelation my sister has never quite forgiven her for.

Thankfully *The Fifth Element* has no late-in-the-third-act twist. Nor does it pretend to be anything other than what it was marketed as. This is an end-of-the-world caper. In space. In the future. With Willis at the helm.

As a thirteen-year-old who'd been brought up on a steady diet of *Star Wars* (before the prequels, I should add), as well as TV shows like *seaQuest DSV* and *Sliders*, this sci-fi spectacle was all I needed for a great time (and hey! it has a discernible female lead, something I've long demanded of the pop culture I consume). In the first forty minutes or so, Luc Besson's film zips and zooms by with teenage abandon. The plot follows the quest to retrieve four sacred stones (or "elements") that, along with the fifth (made flesh in the form of supermodel Milla Jovovich as the character Leeloo), will create a super weapon that'll destroy the evil force-cum-planet that is out to annihilate everything in its path. Recruited to help stop the planet is a toughened former soldier named Korben Dallas (that'd be Willis) who's now working as a New York City cab driver in the year 2263. In the script, Besson describes Korben as "powerfully built," with "unquestionable charm," "good looking in spite of the scars here and there." The first time we meet him he's hazily waking up for yet another day at his dreary job (a downgrade since his decorated military days). His life, and his cramped yet high-tech shoebox of an apartment, have seen better days. He's the film's everyman. If our average everyman wore backless orange tank tops and impossibly tight-fitting pants, that is.

The film is that rare nineties breed of blockbuster that so perfectly balanced self-seriousness and outsized ridiculousness. Where else would you find a committed Gary Oldman sporting a half-shaved look and a horrid triangular soul patch while spouting near-cringeworthy lines like, "You see, Father, by causing a little destruction, I am in fact encouraging life"? The film bears the fact it was originally conceived by Besson when he was just sixteen years old. In contrast with the striking minimalism that was all the rage in dystopian sci-fi spectacles— think of the austere suits of *Gattaca*, the muted color palette of that *Lost in Space* remake, even the black leather getups in the green-tinged *The Matrix*—*The Fifth Element* was an explosion of extravagant style and saturated color. Korben's apartment and flying cab car are spaces filled with useless knobs and endless buttons, a plasticity and tactility that make it feel like Korben and Leeloo have been dropped into life-sized versions of Besson's teenage sketchbooks. Somehow, Janet Maslin calling the film a "gaudy epic" pitched at a "teenage audience that values hot design over plot coherence" in *The New York Times* feels less like a pointed critique and more like an accurate read. Make no mistake, this is a high-octane, high-testosterone ride. It certainly was for me.

But then, at the forty-minute mark, I was stopped in my tracks. It's then when Willis's Korben learns firsthand that Leeloo, nearly naked and recently rescued, doesn't appreciate being kissed while unconscious. She responds to the inappropriate gesture by pointing Korben's own gun at him and uttering something in her language, gibberish to the charming New Yorker. "What does 'Ecto gammat' mean?" asks Korben. It is up to the priest, who's been tasked with gathering the elements to save the world and needed to recruit Korben on this mission, to play real-time translator: "Never without my permission."

In hindsight, I recognize this as a lesson in consent, but I remember audibly groaning at this moment as a teen. Why was this bonkers film about the battle between good and evil careening into romantic territory? Still, my teenage self couldn't help but think, had I been

Leeloo, kissing Korben would have been like waking up to Prince Charming. Who wouldn't want that? Though truly, Korben was light-years ahead of what any fairy-tale Prince Charming could offer. Willis's character, unlike those bland princes, seemed to have a pulse, at least. Upon meeting Leeloo—after she'd jumped from a building and crash-landed on his cab—he'd been struck speechless. "His heart heads for a meltdown," Besson writes in his script. It explains why he so brazenly tries to kiss her, a move film and Leeloo alike do not encourage. Our leading lady is no blushing flower and she sure as hell is no sleeping beauty.

Leeloo does eventually warm up to Korben. Because truly, who wouldn't? The film goes out of its way to make this sly reluctant action hero into a walking sci-fi heartthrob. There is, first of all, the film's unabashed fetishization of Willis's arms. As if echoing his *Die Hard* alter ego, the actor spends much of the film wearing a tank top. Even when he dresses up, his collared shirt gets conveniently torn to look like one, as if his bulging shoulders always need to be set free to better bear the weight of the world. The film may spend plenty of time telling us that Leeloo is "perfect," with many men gawking at her limber body. But it is Willis, sweaty and breathless most of the time, that the camera lingers on.

Costume designer Jean Paul Gaultier didn't hide where his own proclivities lay. Jovovich's sleek, simple steampunk look (white tee, orange suspenders to match her fiery locks) may be iconic, but it's clear that it's the men's costumes the French designer agonized over, finding ways of accentuating biceps, thighs, and backs in surprisingly transgressive ways. Putting Luke Perry in knee-high boots in the opening scene alone was a nineties gay wet dream come true. Gaultier, who's long admitted he first decided to become a fashion designer after watching the 1945 film *Falbalas* as a child, brought his entire designing ethos to *The Fifth Element*. Where his previous cinematic collaboration (with Pedro Almodóvar, in the outrageous

Spanish melodrama *Kika*) had Gaultier grounded in that filmmaker's red-colored, women-led contemporary fantasy, working with Besson gave him carte blanche to let himself imagine a future that was unlike any we'd seen before. As Susan Orlean (yes, *that* Susan Orlean) summed up his fashion career in a profile for *The New Yorker*, "His fantasy world was one where ethnicity and gender were comfortably jumbled—a kimono could be spliced onto a double-breasted suit, or a ball gown could be made of camouflage fabric or, even better, of camouflage fabric that on closer inspection revealed itself to be colored bunches of nylon tulle, a cheap material usually used only for tutus and wedding dresses."

In his work with Willis and Jovovich, you can see Gaultier pushing Besson's testosterone-fueled images into queerer territory. Willis's backless top may have seemed like a novel costuming proposition, but it was already old hat for Gaultier connoisseurs, who'd seen the haute couturier put male models in equally suggestive attire for decades. Back in 1983, in the aptly titled collection "L'homme objet" (often translated as "Boy Toy" but quite literally "The Man Object"—or better yet, "The Male *as* Object"), he'd introduced a backless short-sleeved sweater, a riff on the signature piece that has become almost synonymous with the designer: the striped sailor shirt. This is the Gaultier that I was most aware of growing up. I was never much into high fashion, nor had I yet discovered his collaborations with his long-time friend Almodóvar (if you *must* seek out a Gaultier/Almodóvar collaboration, though, do watch *La mala educación* instead of *Kika*; you'll be rewarded with Gael García Bernal in full drag wearing a sequined nude illusion dress, which is as astounding a moment on-screen as it sounds).

To me, Gaultier was, above all else, a men's fragrance. Not just any fragrance, the one that came in a bottle designed to look like a headless, armless male torso. The blue-hued, striped, statuesque bottle echoed an abstract version of Gaultier's iconic marinière look. But that was only half the story; sold in tin cans that visually called up foodstuffs at sea, Le Male made ample use of sailor imagery in its marketing, a prime example of Gaultier's playful approach toward the modern man. In one of its first ad campaigns, photographer Jean-Baptiste Mondino shot a twinned oiled-up David Fumero arm wrestling with himself, one version in a sailor T-shirt, the other shirtless. There's a performative masculinity at play here, with the tee (a crop top, no less), the sailor hats (perfectly askew, of course), and the laughably obvious bicep tattoos (a roaring feline, a winged heart adorned with the word *love*) softening and eroticizing a classically rugged image of masculine strength. Here was Gaultier's inspiration made flesh.

The sailor motif that's so central to Gaultier has a long (and very queer) history. The French designer has credited Rainer Werner Fassbinder's 1982 film, *Querelle*, for the homoerotic image of the "Handsome Sailor" that's at the heart of Le Male. But, of course, Fassbinder's lurid cult classic about its beautiful titular sailor (played by the drop-dead gorgeous Brad Davis), who seduces camera and characters alike when he's not selling drugs and slicing throats, is a loose adaptation of Jean Genet's underground 1947 novel *Querelle de Brest*, which had, in its first printing, boasted explicit illustrations courtesy of Jean Cocteau. This thieving and murderous protagonist is quintessential Genet, an outlaw that keenly connects the wild adventures at sea with those hustling ones on the streets. With his soiled white turtleneck sweater and his denim pants, Querelle is an imperious and seductive character. He instills lust in Lieutenant Seblon (who's responsible for most of the colorful descriptions of Querelle in Genet's once-banned text), as well as an attendant sense of fear. When he watches Querelle arrive with dirtied pants, he knows better than to reproach him—mostly because the response would be flippantly scathing: "That's just from all the suckers going down on me," Seblon imagines Querelle saying, "While they're giving me a blowjob, they come all over my jeans. That's just their spunk. That's all." Such impudence, as infuriating as it is intoxicating, is key to Genet's protagonist, who hooks you in precisely because he could so easily discard you.

When that first Le Male ad twinned its model and pit him against himself, Gaultier was playing into narcissistic sexual fantasies that the likes of Fassbinder, Genet, and Cocteau—not to mention filmmakers like Kenneth Anger and photographers like James Bidgood—had been keying into for decades, excavating tales of male hustlers and working sailors that painted a picture of men whose ruggedness and latent violence made them entrancing. As one character puts it in Fassbinder's film, "It's difficult to brush past those shoulders, profiles, curls, those strong and supple boys without imagining them capable of murder." The German filmmaker leaned heavily into the porous line between eroticism and violence; Querelle's first murder takes place right after his criminal accomplice strips down to his white briefs as the two discuss the many-varied sexual proclivities that dominate the film. "If you saw my brother," Querelle tells his soon to be victim, "he'd turn you on too. You'd get together with him." At the center of every interaction Querelle has with the men in Brest is the question of manliness. Of how to remain a man when, say, you're fucked by Nono, the bar owner who asks the men who want to fuck his wife to roll dice with him; if they lose, he gets to sodomize them first. "You don't have to prove to me that you're a man," the leather-vest-clad policeman mollifies Querelle as he probes the pretty sailor for details on what happened with Nono after Querelle lost the dice roll, "We know, we're both men."

Querelle, film and novel alike, toys with the trappings of masculinity. You can see how seductive Genet and Fassbinder find these muscled men whose aggression and penchant for violence mark them as the epitome of "real" men. Seen through their eyes, such images become near parodies of themselves, with elements like the sailor outfit (or the leather cap that reads POLICE, say) subjecting these characters to a lustful gaze they invite and abhor in equal measure. Namely, they are every gay male porn fantasy come to life. And, ever the aesthete, this is all telegraphed by Fassbinder's stylish flourishes, including Querelle's own outfit. It's those bell-bottom pants that hug every inch of Davis's lower half. The hat that sits just so on his head. And the low-cut white tank top that frames and draws our eyes to his hairy chest (while its wide racer-back lovingly delineates his every muscle). But then again, all the men in the film are beautiful and Fassbinder's camera lovingly lingers on every one of them, caressing their every oiled-up muscle. This exaltation of the "phallic masculinity" Genet's entire oeuvre celebrates (there was no violent hustler or murderous brute the French novelist couldn't turn into a hero of his own work) gets carried over from Fassbinder's film all the way into Gaultier's fashion.

But even more so than in *Querelle*, Gaultier's ads turn the sailor into an aesthetic. Over the decades as a designer, he's come to deploy these elements of a queered masculinity on the runway and in his advertising campaigns. He put men in skirts in that same "Boy Toy" collection without ever thinking it was a transgressive move. "It was not a gay statement—quite the contrary," he told Orlean. "Men were changing—they were not so macho. So I thought, Why not?"

To see Bruce Willis's Korben Dallas in *The Fifth Element* is to see bits and pieces of what Gaultier had been toying with on the runway and in his ready-to-wear pieces (and what he'd pilfered and refracted in his work from Fassbinder's film), constructing traditional garments yet finding their erotic potential in subtle if unmistakable ways. Gaultier's coup de grace in the film, though, is Ruby Rhod, played by Chris Tucker. The fast-talking Ruby is the biggest radio star in the universe. "It's a great honor to be on his show," an air stewardess tells Korben, unable to contain her excitement when he first shows up halfway through the film. No sooner has Korben tried to wheedle himself out of meeting this famous DJ than Ruby slides into the frame screaming his name, wearing a body-hugging leopard-print blazer-cum-leotard with a plunging neckline. He is flamboyance personified (his peroxide hair is totally tubular, literally). In his review of the film, *Entertainment Weekly*'s Owen Gleiberman derisively described him as "Rodman, Little Richard, RuPaul, and Urkel stirred up in the same cocktail shaker." Damning, though when you think about it, quite accurate praise. The *LA Times* reached for a near identical comparison, pointing out that Ruby "makes RuPaul—or for that matter Dennis Rodman—seem as calm and sedate as Whistler's mother," a reference to the famed James McNeill Whistler painting of his stern-looking mom.

More importantly, though, Ruby is a high-pitched camp queen who breathes more desire into the film than whatever chaste sexual tension was brewing between Korben and Leeloo. Any misgivings one may have about whether the film goes out of its way to sexualize Willis are dispelled once Ruby arrives: "This boy is cuuute," he hisses, "Like fire! So start melting, ladies, because he's hotter than hot!" In a way, his pronouncements are not too dissimilar from the kind that follow Fassbinder's protagonist, whom everyone agrees is a beauty worth pining away for.

The character of Ruby had originally been offered to Prince; Gaultier went so far as to begin dreaming up ideas for his character ahead of a meeting he had with the singer. Only, the iconoclastic artist found Gaultier's designs—which included a mesh bodysuit with clumps of hair sprouting from the arms, chest, and, in a cheeky nod Gaultier has admitted did not tickle Prince whatsoever, from behind—too outré even for him. There's no escaping that the French designer was trying to channel and explode Prince's signature androgynous style in the costumes he'd eventually tailor to Tucker, whose performance teeters between the feminine and masculine undertones of his character's first (ruby) and last (rod) name. Even as he tells his listeners that they'll know everything there is to know about Korben ("his dreams, his desires, his most intimates of intimates"), Tucker is circling another blushing stewardess. He lowers his voice as he whispers in her ear, a seduction by proxy, where Korben is both object and conduit. Besson's script constructs Ruby as a shining example of the unconcern with which this futuristic world understands gender and sexuality.

When faced with films like *Querelle*—or like Genet's own *Un chant d'amour*, which I screened not too soon after reading John Rechy's *The Sexual Outlaw*, thus getting a snapshot education on queer hustling stories as a wide-eyed undergrad whose brush with said encounters IRL only once ever involved a park bench in downtown Vancouver—it can be easy to read what the filmmaker's intent is in, say, letting our eyes linger on a coal-dusted, shirtless Brad Davis. Fassbinder wants you to ogle his every muscle, to think of the labor that's defined his pectorals. Ruby felt like an invitation to do the same with Korben. Except he did so while seducing young women who were agog at the DJ's swagger. I remember watching that early Ruby scene and feeling disoriented for what I thought it was telling me about myself. Did this futuristic dandy give me hope that my own flamboyance was not incompatible with my supposed and compulsory heterosexuality? Or does asking such a question prove that I was looking for ways of deferring an inevitable admission? For, to describe his every outfit is to end up sketching out an effeminacy that was hard to miss (to the opera, Ruby wears a black bodysuit with a dramatic neckline adorned with red roses). And yet this famous futuristic DJ was aggressively heterosexual. But then maybe such a label feels out of place here. Or there, I guess, in the year 2263.

Being so unapologetically flamboyant earned Tucker's Ruby his fair share of scorn from critics. Not just Gleiberman; Maslin describes him as a "yammering, swishy talk show host," while *Variety*'s Todd McCarthy clearly had him in mind when he groaned that "the punkish and gender-crossing orientation of many of the characters looks straight out of any trendy contempo nightclub"; echoing him in *The Hollywood Reporter*, Duane Byrge argued that Gaultier's "outré duds"

here "are off-putting" when not worn by the likes of Naomi Camp-
bell. Reading these reviews all these years later captures the anxiety
I felt upon watching Ruby up on-screen. As a teenager, Ruby Rhod
felt to me like a cartoonish character. One who, like, say, the image
of bejeweled, caped Walter Mercado, made me cower in secondhand
embarrassment. Men who fashioned themselves, in ways both literal
and figurative, as Ruby does, make people uncomfortable. The com-
parisons to RuPaul and Dennis Rodman made it clear that the present
had few acceptable models through which to make sense of a character like him.

To see in Ruby merely an effete clown, a walking stereotype
who was straight-washed so as to make him more palatable to those
testosterone-fueled teens Besson was courting, is understandable.
That's what I felt when I first encountered him. Flamboyance could
only be made legible when same-sex desire was bracketed out of the
equation. And yet there's a more generous reading to be made here,
one that reminds us that uncoupling effeminacy from homosexuality, for instance, is as forward-looking a goal as any other. In the
film, we see Ruby command the room with his sheer presence; he's a
family-friendly icon whom schoolgirls line up to meet for autographs.
In the year 2263, his flamboyance is not just accepted, it is embraced
and celebrated. And rather than neuter him sexually, it emboldens
him. We should be making space, after all, for men to indulge in
their fashionable whims regardless of their sexual orientation. The
femininity Gaultier imbued Ruby with (an inverse, almost, of the
masculinist aggression he'd softened in his sailor imagery) only made
Tucker's performance all the more generative; there's a sense of possibility therein if you know how and where to look for it.

In hindsight, Ruby Rhod feels like the kind of character who
was ever so slightly ahead of his time. To say Ruby walked so Lil
Nas X could run may sound reductive, but there is something to be
said about how the young rapper has handily weaponized the kind of

unabashed effeminacy Tucker's character embodied into a best-selling (and viral-ready) public persona that feels novel precisely because its lineage has been peppered with equally trailblazing exceptions: Rodman and RuPaul but also Prince and Little Richard, as well as Elton John and Freddie Mercury.

This is also what makes Lil Nas X's unapologetic queerness—he's a performer as comfortable reframing the high school locker room as backdrop to a steamy gay hookup as he is wearing silver skirts that show off his toned legs while singing about wanting jet lag from "fucking and flying"—all the more inspiring. Lil Nas X sketches a future my thirteen-year-old self, watching *The Fifth Element* and seeing Gaultier's queer designs fragmented in a sci-fi spectacle anchored by Willis's strong shoulders and Tucker's sibilant *s*'s, couldn't ever have foreseen. There's a sense of humor to the way the "Montero (Call Me by Your Name)" singer revels in the strictures he's called to adhere to, the way only a neon-pink-cowboy-hat-wearing singer could.

As I near forty I've come to realize I can't quite afford to disavow the future, not least because it keeps catching up to me. For no matter how I intellectualize it, looking ahead can never be solely the stuff of children.

What if the future were, could be, queer? Or, in less academic terms, what if our visions for the future could be less unimaginative recreations of our present or imperative templates to be traced but instead occasionally fabulous avenues of thought? I can't, of course, claim such ideas as my own. These are the motivating questions behind José Esteban Muñoz's influential tome *Cruising Utopia: The Then and There of Queer Futurity*. If *No Future* had offered me a life raft in my early twenties, Muñoz's fabulous formulations ("Queerness is a structuring and educated mode of desiring that allows us to see and feel beyond the quagmire of the present," he writes in the opening paragraph) helped anchor me in a much more forward-looking stance in my thirties.

The movies have always been the place where I allow myself to time travel into the future. They needn't always be sci-fi spectacles.

There are times when older films—like, *Querelle,* for instance—feel as forward-thinking as anything featuring flying cars or exploding spaceships. I've never much related to theories that suggest art is there to reflect our lives, a mirror that either shows us who we really are or that helps us see us as we could one day be. There's a rigidity to this formulation; it freezes me in time and similarly mummifies that which is being screened. The moments I've most felt in tune with movie characters is when I've been forced to read against the grain, finding likeness in difference. Those moments where feelings hit home despite the characters on-screen (be they a swishy DJ or a cruising sailor) existed in a world so different from my own that it was only in such unlikely kinship that I realized what it was I was responding to and what it told me about myself. But that would also help me dream of futures and presents free of patriarchal masculinity's tyranny, the kind I've long been pushed to see myself reflected in.

Wanting to wrestle the mirror metaphor away has pushed me to think of alternate formulations that could better capture how we experience those thorny, thrilling moments of recognition. What would it mean, for example, to think of the screen as a lens through which filmmaker and audience in tandem refract one another's experiences, splintering them so as to create new possibilities? What could we imagine if we thought of the screen as a disco ball, reflecting our own light back at us in dizzying new rhythmic compositions that encourage us to dance with abandon? Or a reflecting pond whose ripples we could encourage so as to distort our own images, in turn? Or a prism through which our ideas get filtered, only to emerge all the more changed on the other side?

Maybe this is how we imagine and build our futures, not by being beholden to what they tell us about what's to come, but by embracing the way they can only ever be warnings and lessons of who we are— not mere snapshots of our present selves but a kaleidoscopic vision of who we may already be.

10.

A Cock in a Frock

MARICA. MARICÓN. MARICONADA.

Fag. Faggot. Faggotry.

Even written out like that, I can't help but prefer the English versions. With their swishy *f*'s and plunging *g*'s, there's a typeset flourish to them.

In contrast, those Spanish variations, with their hardened *c*'s, have always felt like tiny pebbles thrown my way, their hurtful impact always dulled and amplified by how carelessly they were deployed in everyday speech. To this day, members of my family continue to use them interchangeably to mean "silly" or "stupid" or "useless." In that sense, a word like *marica* is closer to how *gay* is sometimes used in the United States as a casual (and, to some, simply inadvertent) homophobic put-down. Even in professional settings, I've been told, without a hint of irony or self-awareness, that the use of *marica* in Colombian slang is not really a slur. Not an actual curse word. Just a linguistic tic not worth translating as *fag* lest English speakers reading subtitles get mistakenly offended by what's nothing more than a word casually peppered through otherwise banal dialogue. No worse than, say, *damn* or *jeez* or, yes, *man*.

For years this is how I experienced homophobia at home. Not

171

with any one instance of openly hurtful provocation (though there were plenty of those as well) but with the insistent and incessant monotony of linguistic crutches that eroded any ability to claim those words, let alone those identities, as my own. It's why I found refuge in the English language. It may be an illusory oasis whose own linguistic biases feel, in their foreignness, easier to parse out, discard, or ignore accordingly, but it's nevertheless given me the tools with which to see myself anew.

When I came out to my mother, the words "Soy gay" felt awkward, the expression leaving a chalky taste in my mouth. What was odd in that moment, especially as the world seemed to stand still as my mom's reaction slowly turned from shock and panic to anger and frustration ("What did I do wrong?" she asked herself out loud), was how ill-equipped I felt to handle it in the first place. Not just emotionally but linguistically. I steered clear of words like *marica* (which had always felt like a slur) and *homosexual* (which remains all too clinical), but in grasping for *gay*, I found myself caught between the two languages, one serving as the makeshift bridge I needed to cross this particular hurdle. For, by the time I'd come out in our family's kitchen on a listless Sunday afternoon, I'd had plenty of practice making my sexuality known, in ways explicit and implicit, to friends and colleagues at university in Vancouver. It wasn't just that I was thousands of miles away from anyone who'd known me growing up—I'd given myself the cleanest of slates with which to refashion myself—but that, in shedding Spanish (and the affected lower register my voice instinctively reaches for when I speak it), I could shed the shame instilled in me by those childhood taunts.

I am the first to admit I might not have been as successful as I first thought. Languages have a way of cleaving you in half. Looking back, what I accomplished by owning English labels as liberatory gestures was to ignore the root of the problem altogether; I only found a much more fitting garb for it. But perhaps, as James Baldwin writes, what I have always needed is a less constricting one. "Identity would seem to be the garment with which one covers the nakedness of the self," he writes in *The Devil Finds Work*, "in which case, it is best that the garment be loose, a little like the robes of the desert, through which one's nakedness can always be felt, and, sometimes, discerned. This trust in one's nakedness is all that gives one the power to change one's robes." Put simply, Baldwin reminds us that any identity you may claim (or that may be imposed on you) is layered on yourself. Or rather, on your "self." Think of the labels you use to introduce yourself (*gay*, for example) or the garments you don to make those labels intelligible (a rainbow sweatband, say); they may feel innate, and may very well rub up against your sense of self, but there is, Baldwin cautions and comforts us, a nakedness underneath. One that cannot, of course, be made visible lest you wish to be made vulnerable to the elements (or, if you follow the metaphor far enough, to ogling bystanders). This isn't an outright rebuke of the work identity does, or a mere refusal to acknowledge the way identity makes knowable something about ourselves—after all, tight-fitting garments accentuate different bodies differently while loose-fitting robes have ways of shaping curves and muscles in decidedly varied ways.

There's a call here to think of identity as a robe you cannot only discard and change but can loosen and tighten at will. A fluidity, in fact, that's proffered as not only necessary but unavoidable. But, more intriguingly, I'm always fascinated by the latent eroticism Baldwin calls up, especially when you try to tease out who else may be feeling and discerning your own nakedness. Self-fashioning, it seems, can never stray too far from desire.

What I remember most about coming out to my friends and classmates in Vancouver are my attempts to make such self-disclosure as explicit as could be. Some of that entailed being bold enough to pierce my earlobe (the right one, as I'd heard that's the one gay men sported earrings on), spending way too much money on the kind of bag Jerry Seinfeld would've begrudgingly called a "man purse," and finally purchasing that Jean Paul Gaultier scent whose ads I'd long lusted after. These decisions sound so minor all these years later. But back then, they felt inordinately important. They were a way to signal to others (and myself, more likely) the comfort I felt in crossing lines I'd once been too afraid to even fathom inching close to. That young man who fretted over stealthily buying clear mascara to better accentuate his eyelashes would be shocked at the nonchalance with which I painted my nails and wore a pleated skirt to a Halloween party recently (in itself a minor accomplishment when it comes to occasionally embracing a femme aesthetic). But what was more revelatory was the fact I didn't feel the need to remove my nail polish before traveling home to see my mom (as I've sometimes done in the past). To her credit, though, she did admit my purple-painted nails looked quite nice. Not that I don't struggle still with my knee-jerk reactions at how feminine I sometimes may look or sound. To this day, the memory of a college crush derisively pointing out he could tell it was me walking toward him even at dusk because he could recognize my hips swinging wildly in my Lululemon yoga pants (he didn't care for the strut, less so the getup), pains me still with flickering residual shame.

The friends I made in college, especially those with whom I would come to serve at Pride UBC, the local LGBTQ campus group, broadened my worldview in ways that felt wholly organic at the time but which I realize now were starkly new—and yes, foreign—for a nineteen-year-old Colombian kid who was learning what it was like to not have a school uniform to fall back on. Untethered from my bedroom television and weekend family moviegoing outings, I finally found time to look not (only) to screens to find new models for being and becoming, but to find looser and more fitting robes with which to hide (and maybe discern) my own nakedness. Much of that took place in the privacy of my dorm room, yes, but also in queer

and queer-friendly spaces I'd only ever apprehended on my television
screen from the comfort of my bedroom.

The very first drag show I saw was at a gay club in Vancouver
called The Odyssey. It was Madonna night, an event timed to coincide with the release of the singer's latest release, *Confessions on a
Dance Floor* (the most-played album of my undergraduate years). The
final number of the night was a showstopper that remains, all these
years later, a highlight of my Vancouver nightlife experience (give or
take that time I drunkenly rode a mechanical bull). The song was
"Vogue," of course, and the entire performance was inspired by Madonna's instantly iconic rendition of the hit single at the 1990 MTV
Video Music Awards. Arguably one of the most talked about VMA
performances of all time, the evening found Madonna recasting her
famous ode to the ballroom scene at an eighteenth-century European
court, borrowing freely from images of Marie Antoinette and from
the sultry costumes worn by the Marquise de Merteuil, Glenn Close's
iconic role in Stephen Frears's 1988 hit, *Dangerous Liaisons*. With a
powdered wig, a flouncing skirt, and a fan to match, Madonna held
court with her dancers, turning the song's "Strike a pose!" lyric into
a fabulous indictment of moneyed, royal gentry—all while showcasing dancers like Luis Camacho and Jose Gutierez (and their gorgeous
legs, dressed as they were in tiny golden booty shorts), who'd initially
introduced the "Material Girl" to the world of ballroom and vogueing
back in New York City.

There was a welcome rewriting of the song at work. Ballroom
culture was grounded in parody and impersonation, in exaggerated
fashions and performative exaltations of things coveted and out of
reach. This scene, which went somewhat mainstream with the one-
two punch of "Vogue" and Jennie Livingston's documentary *Paris Is
Burning* in 1990, has a much longer history. The bustling balls in
Harlem, for instance, were already safe havens to queer communities
in the early twentieth century; these were spaces that allowed any

and all sorts of people to commingle and to indulge in all sorts of gender presentation. Already by 1933, when Parker Tyler and Charles Henri Ford published *The Young and Evil*—a modernist novel in the style of their close friend Gertrude Stein that aimed to ethnographically capture the budding queer scene in New York City's Greenwich Village—a Harlem ball was the stuff of legend. When the novel's protagonists (neither "in drag," though one had put on powder-blue eyeshadow, black mascara, and an orange-red rouge on his lips) arrive at this uptown gathering, "the dance-floor," their narrator writes, "was a scene whose celestial flavor and cerulean coloring no angelic painter or nectarish poet has ever conceived." The novel goes on to offer a kaleidoscopic snapshot of the crowd at hand, which defied categorization: "One was with blonde hair and a brown face and yellow feathers and another was with black hair and a tan face and white feathers. Some had on tango things and some blue feathers. One wore pink organdie and a black picture hat." The welcome extravagance Tyler and Ford captured in their dizzying novel could as easily describe any of the balls that have followed in its wake. The quick-witted and stylish patronage *The Young and Evil* depicted ("He had large eyes with a sex-life of their own and claimed to be the hardest boiled queen on Broadway," its narrator notes about Vincent, that night's master of ceremonies) is not too far removed from the instantly quotable world Livingston captured with her cameras in *Paris Is Burning* (as Dorian Corey explains in that doc, "Shade is I don't tell you you're ugly, but I don't have to tell you because you know you're ugly . . . and that's shade") or the balls *Pose* has since fictionalized (not unlike Billy Porter's Pray Tell, Vincent dons a satin blouse and black breeches while overseeing the grand march).

Often referred to as "fairy balls" in the early twentieth century, these events opened up spaces for socially sanctioned cross-dressing, a queering of gender performance away from less prurient and more prescriptive eyes, a space particularly constructed by and for queer folks of color who found refuge in such hallowed halls. "In ballroom, you can be anything you want," Corey says in that 1991 documentary, capturing the imaginative potential of walking in any of the codified categories that by the late twentieth century constituted ballroom competitions. Those attending the balls (many from low-income backgrounds, plenty living on the streets and perhaps even ostracized from their own families) may not be able to get a job as an executive down on Wall Street, but they could walk the "Executive Realness" category, for instance, and let themselves embody that role with abandon. This is why Madonna's "Vogue" performance at the VMAs felt weighted with so many overdetermined meanings: instead of using vogueing as an embodied performance wherein dancers emulate professional models (like those featured in *Vogue* the magazine), and thus presenting an aspirational fantasy of upward mobility, Madonna's staging satirizes trappings of the wealthy. Vogueing demands dancers use their bodies like whips to demand and command attention; transposed to an eighteenth-century royal setting that in itself was a mere performance let Madonna equally revel in and mock aristocratic attitudes as mere poses. It was a reminder of the way drag (and Madonna's exhortation to "strike a pose!") offered a cogent theory of identity as inherently performative—an image made all the more striking by her Marie Antoinette–like costume.

Before that night at The Odyssey, to wit, my only other introduction to drag queens had been through another Madonna TV moment. Back in 1999 the VMAs celebrated her career with a tribute that included a group of drag queens showcasing the singer's iconic looks, including, of course, her "Vogue" ensemble. The moment was punctuated by a deadpan quip delivered by the Material Girl herself after surveying all of her impersonators: "It takes a real man to fill my shoes."

At The Odyssey, in front of a couple of other men trying to fill her shoes, I remember thinking, here was queer artistry at its most elemental. Here was a thrilling and playful rewriting of identity. For someone who'd soon become obsessed with Pedro Almodóvar (thanks in no small part to seeing Gael García Bernal in drag in *La mala educación*) and ABBA (after discovering *Muriel's Wedding* and *The Adventures of Priscilla, Queen of the Desert*, courtesy of an Aussie college boyfriend), these instances of glittering, lived-in revamping of classics with a gender-bending twist (but also, didn't Madge already look like a drag queen in that performance anyway?) established a welcome entry point into a world that would, in a few years' time, go supernova across the border thanks to an at-first quite modest reality TV competition on the fledgling LGBTQ network Logo TV.

On February 2, 2009, the first image that greeted viewers of season one of *RuPaul's Drag Race* was that of a young RuPaul Charles. Recapping his own story for an audience who may not have been privy to his rise from the projects in San Diego, California, to the highest echelons of global stardom in the 1990s, the self-described "Supermodel of the World" hoped to find the next drag superstar in one of the nine queens he'd invited to compete in the inaugural season for his self-titled show. Freely and flagrantly borrowing from ballroom culture (with runway categories), pageant competitions (with a crown and prize money), and revues (with lip sync performances), as well as early 2000s reality television (that freshman season was equal parts *Project Runway*, *America's Next Top Model*, and sometimes even *Fear Factor*), *RuPaul's Drag Race* positioned itself as a purveyor of and platform for drag queen performers all over the country. Not for nothing has Ru often dubbed it the Olympics of Drag.

Appointing himself as the arbiter of contemporary drag in the twenty-first century was an easy pivot for RuPaul. For decades he'd been preaching the gospel of drag, not just as an aesthetic or an art form but as a helpful life philosophy. An ontology, really. His signature line, "We're all born naked and the rest is drag," was more than a cheeky mantra—it has become a call to arms. A call to look at our identity markers as performances—garments, loose- or tight-fitting as they may be, that we wear to project certain aspects of ourselves. Through the 1990s, whenever RuPaul was called to expound on these thoughts (in interviews, on his own talk show), he stressed how the concept of drag was an eye-opening way of understanding our identities. At a more mainstream level, he was getting at something not unlike the academic theories Judith Butler first sketched in their 1990 book *Gender Trouble*, and then famously in 1993's *Bodies that Matter*. Butler's now oft-quoted dictum—"In imitating gender, drag implicitly reveals the imitative structure of gender itself—as well as its contingency"—was radical at the time for the way it centered the practice of drag in the ways we should and could understand gender performance. It's not that Butler believed gender was all about clothing but rather that, seeing the effect, say, a pair of heels, a blond wig, and a red corset could have on how we responded to a six-foot-four Black man from San Diego, meant that there was maybe more to gender than meets the eye. Or rather, that what meets one's eyes can be equally deceiving and revealing about how we understand gender. Which is not to say early-nineties Ru, or other drag queens, were all consciously trying to make any kind of grand statement about men and women, masculinity and femininity.

But RuPaul's own public image journey in that decade pushed viewers to demystify what drag was all about, to get under its skin, in fact. By the time he published his candid 1995 memoir, *Lettin It All Hang Out*, he was already trying to express how much their own drag was akin to other people's work attire. He may resort to superhero rhetoric when explaining what happens when he spends hours painstakingly putting on his face ("it felt like Clark Kent turning into Superman," he's often said about the very first time he got into drag—and every time since), but in explaining it to others, he's had to put drag in more ordinary terms. When he gets into the Glamazon drag he's now well-known for, it's no different than when an executive puts on a suit or a nurse puts on her scrubs. It's a uniform. "And, like all professionals, I love my uniform," he writes. But in that similarity, Ru reads a lesson to be learned; everything else we put on is a kind of drag. Drag queens just make that all the more self-evident. This is perhaps why RuPaul's own twist on drag eventually catapulted this once marginal and marginalized endeavor into the mainstream.

Like RuPaul's own idol, Oprah, whose career he'd always hoped to emulate, the now Emmy-winning host has successfully packaged a welcome vision of self-help that's rooted in the art of drag. This conviction has become foundational to how Ru markets himself. "It's kind of an existential vision," he told *Interview* magazine about how he thinks of his own performative persona, "and it has to do with breaking the fourth wall and seeing yourself from outside of yourself. That's my drag." It's not just about putting on a dress and walking in heels. It's about what looking at yourself anew in such trappings does to your self-image. As he'd explained in his memoir, "You see, clothes aren't just things you wear—they bring out the flavor of the person, magnifying hidden areas of your personality that spend most of the time cooped up in the cellar of your consciousness. From time to time you need to take them out for a walk around the block." In RuPaul's conceptualization, these are not parts of yourself you're creating out of whole cloth. You're excavating them. Or recovering them. And some-times, nurturing them out of the darkness and into the light of day. These musings—which sometimes feel like trite self-help sound bites at best and like hackneyed TV catchphrases at worst—are familiar to anyone who's ever watched an episode of *RuPaul's Drag Race*. The long-running show is the purest distillation of RuPaul's philosophy of drag, which has, in Butlerian fashion, come to present a welcome fluidity when it comes to thinking through gender and desire.

An early decision that has encouraged this palimpsestuous un-derstanding of gender is the choice to have all contestants present themselves and address one another by their given drag names. And so, while Shannel was the first queen to walk into the show's Werk Room, that's not how they introduced themselves to the camera. "My name is Brian. I am twenty-five years old," a mop-haired young man wearing a black button-up shirt tells the camera in a confessional. "My persona has always tried to be a little more on the realistic side," he explains as we see shots of Shannel surveying the Werk Room in a long-sleeved, low-cut bodysuit and a pair of assless zebra pants, "but wearing costuming that's super couture." It's why he's known as "the Barbra Streisand of drag," he boasts. This is how the season one contestants all introduced themselves, giving audiences their real names before, variously, talking about their stage names, their personas, their alter egos, their characters, or their drag names, making clear distinctions between the two. "I could do things as Victoria that I could never do as Victor," one shares; "Basically she has more balls than I do," another adds.

This may sound like a minor detail, one driven more by the production's continuity concerns than by any gender theorizing, but it's one that's connected every moment a contestant is on-screen to their own drag performance. As Tom Fitzgerald and Lorenzo Marquez note in *Legendary Children*, an encyclopedic look into the show's first decade on air, the choice to show contestants out of drag is an integral part of *Drag Race*'s appeal: even as seeing queens in their "boy drag" was once, as they explain, deemed controversial ("They never want you to see the hand up Kermit's butt," the authors quip), this aspect of the show was key to what Ru was trying to create. "Stripping away the drag is very much of a piece with the show's commitment to showing its full art, which you truly can't appreciate fully without seeing the transformation in process," they further explain. "It's also a way of peeling away any emotional barriers or protections." Part of that stripping away required turning the spotlight onto the backstage to make these performers reality TV contestants.

In live appearances—be they at drag brunches or at bars late into the night, at revues in theaters or at Vegas shows on the Strip—the stage delimits the space where a drag queen performs. The person who donned a wig, some lashes, and a pair of heels (and, as we've seen on the show, plenty more) was always off-screen. RuPaul himself had to make a conscious choice to show people what he looked like out of drag even before *Drag Race* in order to avoid being reduced to what, at the time, his manager dubbed "the Disney version of Ru": "I'm at a point where I want to explore different parts of myself," RuPaul shared in a famed cover story in *The Advocate* in 1994, "I want to make myself known in the public eye out of drag." It was as much a canny professional move as it was a personal one. And it's one he then imported into his reality competition show. Audiences and contestants alike see RuPaul both in and out of drag in every *Drag Race* episode, and so too would they come to see the hundred-plus queens that have walked in his wake in the years since.

But if RuPaul has given us a chance to see him in both "boy drag" and "Glamazon" drag, he's never inhabited the liminal space he's constructed for the queens. You either see RuPaul in a colorful, patterned suit with flashy accessories and eye-catching eyewear with the occasional hat talking to the queens in the Werk Room, or you see Ru sporting a Zaldy original gown that fits like a glove paired with a perfectly coiffed wig and a mug to match on the runway where the judging takes place. But you never see the in-between. His queens may be required to address one another by their drag names, but you also see them transform into those same drag personas. A drag queen on this show necessarily gives up a degree of their allure, of their privacy; their boy looks and their drag looks end up existing alongside one another in a decidedly novel way, like superimposed images that create a hologram effect for viewers watching at home. That the last decade of *Drag Race* has coincided with the explosion of digital media, with YouTube channels, OnlyFans accounts, and Instagram profiles, has only fueled this further, blurring what in those live performance spaces were (and remain, in many ways) clearly delineated public and private spheres. In bringing the backstage onto the stage, as it were, *Drag Race* has built an arena where the fluidity of gender presentation is front and center, even as rigid ideas of masculinity and femininity lord over every critique.

Over the years, and as the show has found not only a wider audience but has also welcomed a broader variety of contestants (including trans women, trans men, bioqueens, and even a straight cis man in its fourteenth U.S. season), *RuPaul's Drag Race* has found the queens both stretching the limits of "femininity" on the runway while chiseling away at notions of "masculinity" in the pink Werk Room. Rather than posit these as distinct categories, spaces to be inhabited and shuttled between, the structure of the show presents (at times fleeting) moments where you watch them be disassembled and reassembled in the blink of an eyelash. Watching a muscle-building queen with tattoos slink her way through a Lizzo song in a crop-top two-piece and a flouncing blond wig or watching a fashion queen opt to use gray wizardly facial hair as a welcome runway prop have turned those neat categories upside down. Even the mere sight of queens out of drag—some in high-femme garments, others in "boy" drag (with painted-on eyebrows, say, or the suggestion of facial hair), others still in more genderless fashion—is enough to dismantle any notion of what a queen looks like when she's not wholly made-up.

What RuPaul has long demanded of his contestants is a kind of inside and outside performance. Drag isn't a mask. It's a window into someone's interiority. When, from the judging table, Ru demands the queens show him who they *really* are, he's asking them to find in their performative postures (and their wigs and dresses, their runway presentations and affectations) a kernel of truth to shine through. Drag as self-disclosure is a kind of counterintuitive idea. One that's cost many a queen the crown. But it's at the center of everything Ru conceives of as drag. Of course, at a meta level, the competition is necessarily requiring its contestants to offer similar self-disclosures when they're out of drag—and more often than not, when they're getting *into* drag. The most affecting moments in *Drag Race* history happen during those vulnerable moments when the queens, as they paint their faces in front of a two-way vanity mirror, share their most intimate secrets with one another—and the show's audience, in turn.

No episode of the show better captures Ru's stalwart belief in drag's emancipatory potential than the one featuring drag makeovers. The goal of such a challenge (a hallmark of the franchise from the very beginning) has always been to get the queens to properly distill their own "brand" of drag and translate it onto a willing volunteer; it's why Ru and fellow judge Michelle Visage stress the importance of showing a "family resemblance" when walking the runway, something that rests as much on makeup and wardrobe as it does on flair and personality. Over the years, the challenge has involved family members, eliminated queens, social media influencers, the show's own crew, and even the stars of *Little Women: LA*. But consistently during its first few seasons, this challenge seemed tailor-made to highlight the absurdity of gender norms. It explains why they were regularly prefaced with ridiculous mini challenges that asked the queens to muster the masculinity their drag personas necessarily suppressed. In season one, for instance, Ru introduced a group of female fighters who then staged an impromptu boxing exercise where the queens' daintiness (even out of drag) was starkly juxtaposed with the bodies and attitudes present courtesy of Krav Maga trainers, Brazilian capoeiristas, and cage fighters. In season three, before bringing in the group of muscled jocks the queens would later make over, Ru proudly unveiled the "Badonkadonk Dunking Machine" in what was clearly a parking area outside the studio. There, we got to witness the queens out of drag try their hand at the carnival staple all while resorting to some hilarious put-downs ("She throws like a girl!" "The harder you throw, the more you look like a dude, that's all I'm saying!") that singled out the sheer absurdity of the endeavor, all while exemplifying the gender-bending humor the game keenly depended on. These mini challenges (which have also included a brutal boot camp, a photo shoot using prison uniforms, and an ad for a cologne named Trade) serve as foils to the makeover challenges, calling for butch imagery and "masc" behavior in a show that most values and privileges fishy femininity, no matter how narrow such a definition of drag that may be.

Alongside the main makeover challenge, RuPaul has often asked her queens to create mini performances on the main stage, getting the paired queens and their made-over partners to produce everything from a safe-sex cheerleading routine to a sexy striptease number. These moments were designed, yet again, to play up archly stylized "feminine" types: hot jocks and handsome DILFs wouldn't just need to look like "real" women but move like them (for a gawking crowd). This all kept with RuPaul's conviction of drag's purpose. "My drag is less about looking like a woman," he writes in his 2018 book, *GuRu*, "and more about saying F.U. to the cult of systematic masculinity I was bombarded with as a little boy." What better way to do it than to force "manly" men who'd otherwise scoff at walking in heels and wearing makeup to drag themselves up and have their transformation be judged by Ru and the world at large?

And therein lies the appeal of the makeover challenge. Rooted in Ru's wholehearted belief in drag as a welcome endeavor that can help anyone and everyone tap into the femininity they're constantly called to dull within themselves, these makeovers invite the show's guests to leave their inhibitions behind and embrace their inner drag queen. Ru constantly frames it in these terms: "This is your chance to reveal the secrets of drag," he tells his queens, "something every real woman should know." Such a concept is what's been at the center of the show's most notable spinoffs, *RuPaul's Drag U* and the star-studded *RuPaul's Secret Celebrity Drag Race*, as well as the HBO docuseries *We're Here* hosted by three of *Drag Race*'s most famous alumni—all of which depend on the didactic potential of drag for anyone brave enough to follow in Ru's and her queens' footsteps.

When I first started watching *Drag Race* (during a blissful, sex-fueled weekend with a friend I'd long had a crush on and whom I've barely seen since), what most intrigued me was the show's ability to create, almost in spite of itself, an environment where the fluidity of gender and sexuality was both taken for granted and celebrated. I say "almost in spite of itself" because, especially in its earlier seasons, the competition was grounded in laughably rigid conceptions of femininity and masculinity, with little room for their in-between. In that very first makeover challenge, for instance, Ru and the judges harshly critiqued Ongina for wearing pinstripe pants with a white halter top on the runway. As the Filipina queen explained, cannily keying into the substance if not the purpose of the challenge at hand, she had hoped to capture a mixture of masculine and feminine in the outfits she presented alongside her fighting partner (who wore a long pinstripe skirt and matching blouse). Later, while the queens relaxed backstage, the judges' critiques got at the tension between what Ongina had aimed for and what had been expected of her: "Ongina looked a little more boyish than usual," one posited, as images of the bald petite queen strutting down the runway flashed across the screen. "A woman in a pantsuit is really great," former *Project Runway* finalist and judge Santino Rice added, "a drag queen in a pantsuit not tucking, is . . . a man." These throwaway comments eventually landed the fan-favorite queen in the bottom two and had her, in the show's lingo, "sashaying away" at the end of the episode. It is but a single example of how Ru and the judges pushed the queens, especially in these makeover challenges, to adhere to a specific brand of fishy femininity, where the illusion of passing as a (beautiful, it must be added) woman was, it seemed, always the goal. This usually left attempts to queer such a concept, like Ongina's wig-less pantsuit ensemble, on the cutting room floor.

In this, *RuPaul's Drag Race* was merely repackaging the way drag had often been explored in mainstream pop culture. Cross-dressing comedies like *Tootsie* and *Mrs. Doubtfire* (both, not coincidentally, centered on hapless straight men who put on a wig and a dress to sidestep obstacles in their professional and personal lives, respectively) posit that there's a thing or two men can learn from walking a mile in a woman's high-heeled shoes. Even comedies about queens—like *The Adventures of Priscilla, Queen of the Desert, The Birdcage,* and, much later, *Kinky Boots*—centered on the power of drag, pitching its self-improvement appeal as well as its eye-opening potential to those less tolerant and accepting. This perhaps spoke more of the expectant audience these projects hoped to cater to than any kind of progressive political idealism. Drag, in these cases, always felt like a plot point that pushed outward, from the fringes of where it lived toward the more acceptable generic confines of the comedic family (melo)dramas that housed them: in *Priscilla,* the narrative engine is a years-old marriage (and a secret son) that prompts a fab ABBA-fueled Aussie road trip; *The Birdcage* is a family farce about a brat of a son who's now embarrassed about his parents' drag revue show; while *Kinky Boots* finds a young entrepreneur trying to save his father's shoe factory with the help of a statuesque drag queen and a welcome niche market.

Of these films, my favorite has always been Stephan Elliott's *Priscilla,* and I'm not afraid to admit that much of that preference stems from my feelings toward Guy Pearce. No offense to the incomparable Terence Stamp or the hilarious Hugo Weaving, the two emotional anchors of this warmhearted film. But I can't deny that sometimes my shallowness (or my horniness, more like) gets the best of me: seeing Pearce, in a black bob, wearing an outfit made entirely of pearls, was the first time I'd found myself so attracted to a drag performer. It helps that later in the film we see him wearing even less, the camera letting us admire his toned ass and abs, his bulging biceps and pecs, as he parades himself, variously, in denim cutoffs, mesh vests, chaps, sleeveless crop tops, and boxer briefs with abandon. Weaving's Tick is a mess of insecurities (if an ebullient bundle of expressivity as Mitzi onstage); throughout the film we find him grappling with what his newfound role of father means for his sexual identity, not to mention his career as a drag queen ("What the hell *are* we?" Pearce's Felicia asks him in exasperation. "I don't fuckin' know!" he replies). Stamp's Bernadette, on the other hand, has a droll, deadpan presence in and out of drag; adrift after losing her partner, this poised trans woman clearly cut her teeth navigating unwelcome spaces. In contrast, Pearce's Adam (aka Felicia Jollygoodfellow), the youngest of the trio, is its most flamboyant. A swishy, bitchy muscled waif of a queen, he's the new vanguard, blissfully oblivious to the fights the likes of Tick and Bernadette had to wage, yet all too happy to reap their benefits. He's also, of course, impossibly attractive (Pearce had gotten his start on Aussie soaps for a reason). In *Drag Race* terms, he could easily have been cast as either part of RuPaul's "Pit Crew" (the group of oiled-up, underwear-clad men who serve as props for many of the show's challenges) or one of the queens gunning for the crown. His cockiness is what keeps him on bad terms with Bernadette, who relishes cutting him down to size whenever she can, most pointedly when Adam shares his desire to climb atop Kings Canyon in full drag: "That's just what this country needs," Bernadette snipes at him, "a cock in a frock on a rock."

My attraction to Adam (not unlike the kind Patrick Swayze inspired in *To Wong Foo, Thanks for Everything! Julie Newmar*, another film about drag queens, featuring an iconic Ru cameo) is rooted, I know, in the exaltation of the masculine beauty of the (yes, very straight) actor who plays him. Pearce's cheekbones alone—not to mention his butt cheeks—have rarely looked as enticing as they do here, both in and out of drag. And it is pertinent that I knew (and know) that Pearce is a straight actor. To see him take on the affectations of Felicia, watch him dole out zingers at the crowd ("Do you know why this microphone has such a long cord? So it's easily retrieved after I've shoved it up your ass," he jeers at a heckler), and witness him swing his hips while christening the titular bus with a bottle of champagne is a kind of (drag) performance in itself. The kind *Drag Race* demands of its volunteers during those makeover challenges. In fact, to hear Al Clark, the film's producer, tell it, the actual casting of the film was designed with similar intent in mind.

Getting three straight actors (including an actor best known then for playing General Zod in the 1978 Superman films and, crucially, as the titular sailor in 1962's *Billy Budd*) for the role of three ABBA-lip-syncing queens wasn't an accident. This was by design. Explaining the exhaustive casting process that preceded the guerrilla-style shoot in the Australian desert in his book *Making Priscilla*, Clark admits he and Elliott had, at the outset, "many frivolous casting ideas—which mostly involve[d] getting particular media celebrities, chat show hosts and folk heroes to make sequined fools of themselves." There was mischief here but also a familiar titillation; as *Drag Race*'s makeover challenges remind us time and again, there's nothing funnier than a butch man in full drag (and nothing quite as impressive either, when such drag is done well). The casting philosophy was to get actors to play "against type." This became necessary when an alleged drag casting call led nowhere; what they'd need was big names, a big draw. And that, given the state of the film industry in the 1990s, left little room for folks from the LGBTQ community. Which is why names such as Jaye Davidson (who'd earned an Oscar nomination for playing a trans woman in *The Crying Game*) and Julian Clary (the self-described "renowned homosexual" comedian) were off the table; and while Rupert Everett was almost signed on to play the role of Tick, Clark explained that, "If we had been making this as a studio picture thirty years earlier, we would have offered the leading roles to people like Burt Lancaster, Lee Marvin and Steve McQueen, the kind of testosterone-saturated actors who are now an endangered if not extinct species." Clark almost sounds like Myra Breckinridge, bemoaning the lack of capital-*M* "Men" in Hollywood's contemporary firmament, all while suggesting their attendant emasculation ("making sequined fools of themselves") is what would give *Priscilla* its main selling point if not its entire raison d'être.

The frisson Clark and Elliott chased after was also there in how the trio of actors approached the material. Ahead of their grueling shooting schedule, Weaving, Stamp, and Pearce all went out to a club called DCM. In full drag. And, true to what Ru's long preached, the three performers used the opportunity to explore what was there all along, finding fodder with which to craft their respective characters. "It is striking what an effect the disguise of drag is having on their personalities," Clark recounts. Pearce, he notes, who'd already been abusing everyone and demanding drinks "as a reward for his unpleasantness," got ever more flirtatious, combative, and loud as the night went on. He may as well have been describing many of the straight men *RuPaul's Drag Race* has made over through the years. Some, perhaps most famously season nine's "Wintergreen" (aka Sarge, from the show's crew), became as sassy as any of the queens on the runway. Others, like "Dad I'd Like to Frock" Mike in season four, equated having a "diva bitch attitude" with cussing out the show's contestants (and protesting, when they cussed back, that there was too much testosterone in the room). Yet as with Felicia in *Priscilla*, the moments I find most revealing in those episodes are the ones where that flirtatiousness comes to the forefront. "You probably have a stiffy down there," guest judge Sharon Osbourne ribbed one of the jocks on the runway who did, in fact, cop to being turned on by himself. In that same episode, Visage point-blank asked another one if they'd date themselves. "Yes. Hard," they replied.

The need to bring desire into these situations reveals how intertwined our concepts of gender and sexuality remain—even, or especially, in a space as all-encompassing as the *Drag Race* stage. It's hard to disentangle one from the other, especially when we're so inclined to think of them in tandem: what men want and what men look like aren't questions to be asked in a vacuum. They are mutually constructive. As Butler points out, there is "no quick or easy way to separate the life of gender from the life of desire." Such a line is instantly legible when you see a queen, out of drag, fanning themselves when the Pit Crew walks in wearing impossibly tight underwear meant to accentuate their every curve. You get it when a straight guest judge can't help but fawn over a fishy-looking queen on the runway or when a queen, in full coquettish mode despite wearing nothing more than sweats and a tank top, blushes when a cute choreographer is barking orders at her. You feel its effect when glances across the room between two queens suggest there may be more than mere camaraderie happening off camera. You can't mistake it when talk of the "trade of the season" takes over the conversation or when a queen's confidence ends up being directly proportional to how in drag (how in character) they feel. The fluidity of their pronouns and gender presentations do more to advance Ru's "we're all born naked" truism than anything that happens on the actual runway. In—but especially out of—drag, many contestants have collectively pushed back against notions that to be effeminate is a fallibility for a man. On the contrary, femininity, in and out of drag, is, most always for these queens, a kind of armor. A source of strength. Not one that denigrates their own sense of manhood but one that coexists alongside it in complementary, and at times incompatible, ways. They may be queens but not for that are they any less men.

For my thirty-seventh birthday I bought myself a white T-shirt with one colorful word splashed across it: MARICÓN. Created by Cachorro Lozano, a Spanish visual artist whose freehand words are made to look like something written out in crayon, the tee was my one attempt at trying to reclaim that word for myself. I hoped it would help me dispel the negative connotations and the many shameful images it's always conjured up in my mind. If in my childhood and teenage years that word had been a nagging pebble thrown my way, I wanted to reclaim it in my mind, in my mouth. To turn it into a kind of defensive weapon of my own. Wearing it out in public that first time was an unnecessarily frightening prospect. Slurs, after all, have a way of getting away from us even when we deploy them ourselves. I saw some people wince when they finally read it, those who understood what it meant, at least, while others did so when I proceeded to explain it. It maybe wasn't as dramatic as a cape (it definitely didn't have as florid a flourish), but emblazoned on my chest the word did give me a jolt of strength. Even when I type it out now, the word forces inadvertent flashes of shame-riddled images: of comedians lisping their way through a bit about sissies, of schoolmates spewing it my way while limping their wrists in unison, of sexually neutered stereotypes on-screen flailing their way through a groan-worthy punchline, of pathetic and unlovable men pining away for burly men who'd never love them. And there's more. Plenty more. Decades more of images and connotations and prejudices and scenarios and jokes and taunts and gestures that hover at the edge of my consciousness whenever I sound the word out loud.

And at its core was a lesson I'm still working to unlearn: that you can't be a man if you are a maricón. That to want a man is to forgo being a real one. It's such simple arithmetic and yet it requires so much theoretical acrobatics. The kind that would be too exhausting to untangle were it not always presented as merely commonsensical. Not that us queer boys have any other choice. Our mere existence demands we examine those early lessons and, if we're lucky, dispense with the lot that once so oppressed us, that once so shamed us in hopes we'd dim ourselves in their wake. That's perhaps why so many of us cherish the beacons that help guide us on our way out of such darkness, who proffer us alternatives that are alluring precisely because they feel so self-evident.

Like much of my queer education, drag has always come my way filtered through the screen. This has meant I've always had both a much closer and a much more removed vantage point from which to understand it. The manufactured intimacy a show like *Drag Race* creates, though, has served as a welcome window into a kind of queer utopia, a space where bodies aren't sites of contention but sites of artistry and possibility. A space where, following Ru's cosmology, we're all encouraged to break masculinity apart, not because it needs to be destroyed but because it deserves to be exploded and extended—to have it be expansive enough to embrace the many multitudes it has always contained.

Acknowledgments

This book has been a long time coming. In many ways I started it as a teenager when I daydreamed about the way men's bodies on screens made me feel. It simmered in college when reading books like John Rechy's *The Sexual Outlaw* opened my eyes to what queer writing could feel like (eternal thanks to Stephen Guy-Bray, whose classes and witticisms have stayed with me these many years later). And it further developed in grad school where reading *Myra Breckinridge* (thank you, Josh Gang!), James Baldwin, and plenty more seminal texts of cultural criticism helped me home in on what's since become a life-long dedication to the sinuous inner workings of queer desire. And so, thanks must be paid to mentors and professors like Elin Diamond, David Kurnick, Carolyn Williams, Marianne DeKoven, and Rebecca Walkowitz, whose classes, feedback, and encouragement pushed my thinking into ever broader territory, even once it was clear academia would not be for me.

But the book, as it exists now, began in earnest during my stint at the Sundance Institute's 2019 Documentary Edit and Story Lab, where the work of wildly talented nonfiction filmmakers inspired me to finally set about drafting my thoughts on masculinity and pop culture into a coherent project (an effort that culminated at a welcome writing retreat in 2020 in Palm Springs hosted by my dear friends, Steven Rowley and Byron Lane). With the encouragement of my then-husband Matt, without whom I'd never have embarked on such a Herculean effort, that decades-old seedling of an idea became ever more real.

The writing of a book, at times thought to be a solitary endeavor, can only ever take place amid a comforting sense of community. In my case, there are friends and colleagues who have offered support in countless ways over the years and who should know how instrumental they've been in helping me get this deeply personal treatise out into world during a truly trying time. Thank you to Brian Pietras, Kyle Stevens, Thad Nurski, Aaron Ahedo, Jeff Ling, Peggy Truong, Jack Smart, Chad Sell, and Stephen Hayes for their patience, care, and attention through these past few years. And thank you to editors like Vanessa Erazo, Matthew Brennan, Jess Zimmerman, and B. Ruby Rich, who have made my writing stronger every time I've worked with them. And particularly to Matt Ortile, who was instrumental in helping me coalesce some of these ideas into self-revealing essays as we worked on my *Catapult* magazine column, "Movie Made Gay."

Thanks must also be extended to my fearless agent Michael Bourret, a champion of this book from the get-go, my editor Alicia Kroell, whose insight and feedback made it all the stronger, Jack Manning for the gorgeous author photo, and the entire Catapult team for their tireless work in giving the book the sexiest cover I could've asked for.

And lastly, thank you to Joe & Ami, for gazing at me in ways I continue to find equally thrilling and inspiring.